"This is one of the most moving and courageous stories I have ever read. The experience of watching the love of your life die must be extraordinarily harrowing. The fact that both Tanya and her husband documented what they were going through during his last days must surely be the staunchest gift to anyone else facing the same experience. This is a love story beyond parallel."

—ANN ANDREWS
AUTHOR

Unplanned Journey

A Triumph in Life and Death

Unplanned Journey

A TRIUMPH IN *Life* and *Death*

TANYA M. UNKOVICH

VMI PUBLISHERS • SISTERS, OREGON

Unless otherwise indicated, Bible quotations are taken from the *Life Application Bible, the Living Bible,* (third Edition), copyright © 1988 by Tyndale House Publishers, Inc.,Wheaton Illinois.

Published by
VMI Publishers
Sisters, Oregon
www.vmipublishers.com

ISBN 13: 9781933204758
ISBN: 1933204753
Library of Congress Control Number: 2008941260
Printed in the USA

This is for you my angel.

May perpetual light shine upon you.

CONTENTS

Preface

It was my husband's 48th birthday on which Phil was informed
by his doctor that he had cancer. The diagnosis was yet unclear; it was
either Lymphoma or Small Cell Carcinoma, neither of which meant anything to us apart from that C word and of this we were certain.

Very shortly after his diagnosis Phil had made the decision to write a
book about his journey and recovery from cancer. It became his passion
and strong desire to share with the world how to conquer this massive
mountain that was placed before him; he strongly believed that with faith
and hope miracles do happen.

Coincidentally Phil began to keep a journal some months before he
was diagnosed and then continued to document his story far more extensively as material for his book. The nature of his writing changed as the
months passed. They began as notes on leadership styles extracted from
his favourite books, to being more of content of his day, then to an expression of his deepest feelings whilst processing what was happening to him
and finally, heartfelt prayer to his God.

Holding onto this passion to write his book was an incentive for Phil
to keep up his fighting spirit and to one day be able to say that he survived
cancer.

Even on the final day of his life, lying in the hospital bed and being
told that he would not leave this bed, Phil turned to me and said, "Don't
forget to bring in my journal tomorrow Tarn as this will be good for my

book." This was the depth of faith that Phil continued to have and would not give up under any circumstance.

Within days of Phil's funeral I developed a deep knowing that it was I who would be fulfilling his dream and telling the story of his journey.

My intention is for you to get to know Phil as I write this story as he was a man whom I and others continue to describe as one in a million. You did not need to spend much time with Phil to be touched in some way by who he was as a fellow human, and this imprint is what I believe will remain with you as you read his words.

Throughout these pages, from Phil's words and my own, you will walk beside us and experience how it was for us both during those five months and also how it was for me during the first year following his death. It is my wish that from this story you will also discover how goodness can come from what at times felt like the deepest depression.

Much of the story has been put together from Phil's journal and my own extensive journal that we both kept during this time. Journaling has been a part of my life since my teenage years; it still is in fact and has been a major contributing factor to my continued healing whilst on this path, one I would often describe as pure horror.

This was not supposed to happen in my life. As a little girl my dream was to get married one day, to have babies and to have my home with the white picket fence and live a happy life. There were to be no glitches in this picture of mine as in my innocent youth, and with the gift of naivety, I did not yet understand that what accompanied the joys of life were also times of unhappiness and sorrow.

Never would I have believed that I would once again find somewhere deep within a willingness to continue with the remainder of my life, to experience joy again, to eventually be able to say that this experience, whilst it has been my most traumatic, has also been my greatest gift.

What originally began as a desire to fulfil Phil's passion of writing a book about his journey has now in fact become my greatest passion. When the time came my words began to flow and what accompanied these words were my tears. During the past twelve months there has been nothing in my world that has given me a greater meaning and purpose to life than completing this book.

Today I feel at peace with our separate journeys knowing that they were both triumphant in their own different ways. Phil triumphed in death, and I, in life.

Acknowledgements

There are so many beautiful people who assisted Phil and me during the five months of his illness and who have continued to support me since his passing and during the many hours of writing this book. Where do I begin to thank you all as the numbers are endless?

Every day I continue to say thank you for my loving parents, Pavica and Smiljan Unkovich. Thank you mum and dad for the sacrifices you have made in your life for the love of your children. You embraced "Philipi" as your own son and showed him unconditional love and kindness as you do for everyone else in your lives.

Thank you to my brothers Zeljan, Nick and Antoni, my sister-in-law Delwyn and my many nieces and nephews. I am so blessed to have such a wonderful family. Zel and Delwyn you embraced me with love and welcomed me into your own family. You were there for Philip constantly and you have stood by your word when Phil asked you to take care of his girl. Nick, you have continued to make us all laugh yet at the appropriate times come out with such wisdom that only you knew how. Antoni, I thank you for rushing to my side in a moment's notice and for being my friend and confidant. I love you all so much.

Thank you to my extended family on Philip's side of the family tree, big sis,' Marie and Neil, Norma and Bill and all of whom there are so many to name, thank you. Marie and Neil, you were Phil's treasure, and I thank you for continuing to embrace me as your little sis.

To my friend Catherine Johnston, where do I begin to thank you? For twenty years you have walked beside me and demonstrated what a true friend is through your constant kindness. You Catherine I am able to describe in one word, which is Love.

My therapist and friend David Chaloner, you rock DC and have been a gift to both Phil and myself. From the time I walked into your rooms all those years ago you have patiently watched and waited as this stubborn Croatian woman finally got it! Phil held a great respect for you and I could not have asked for anyone better to assist me through this time.

To the parish priest Monsignor Cronin and members of the Parish of Sacred Heart in Ponsonby: you are what I called my prayer warriors, and I am privileged to belong to such a family. Father I thank you for being there for us both during Phil's illness and for demonstrating to myself what faith really means.

I am fortunate to have wonderful colleagues and friends in the helping profession who have walked beside me during the highs and lows of my grief process and the forming of this book. A special thank you to you for believing in my vision: Shirley Watkins, Sheryl Madden, Graham Mead, Jill Dunn, Lou Chapman, Carol McMillan, Hazel Mae and Kay Douglas.

Each of my friends are stars, and I feel such gratitude to be surrounded with the most supportive loving group of people. You were there for Phil and I, and you have continued to be by my side during my darkest hour and continue to assist me in finding my way in this world again. I love you guys: Michele Comeau, Sue and Darren Murray, Neecie Moore, Carolyn Boell, Michelle Burgess, Tina Alach and Marko Otis, Ivan and Vesna Druskovich and family, Jo Murphy, Lois and Allan Phillips, Meg Rogers, Ursula and Leanne, David and Danielle Hows, Rosalind Stewart, Tony Hayes, Michele Urlich, Rhona Levenberg, Mike and Sandy Dwyer, Lance and Denise Revill, Cliff McChesney, Rose Gambitisis, David and Karen Chambers, Milly and Vidak Franich.

Thanks to you Fergus, my faithful cat who somehow always knew when I needed snuggles.

Heavenly Father, it never ceases to amaze me of the wonder of Your plan. My path in life has been extraordinary. You have gently prepared me for every trial which I have had to face.

Phil and I had no doubt that you were carrying us during those final five months of his earthly life, and I have never doubted that in spite of my grief you would be with me through this also.

Thank you for placing such a beautiful man in my life as my experiences and memories of Phil will be within me until my final breath. How privileged I feel to have experienced the infinite love that you have for me whilst enduring a journey of such pain. This may I never forget.

PART ONE

Phil's Journey

ONE

November 8, 2004

It was November 8, 2004; we were at my mom and dad's home to celebrate Phil's birthday, just the four of us that night. My parents were not aware that Phil and I were awaiting the results of a biopsy on a lump in his left armpit, a procedure that had been done some five days earlier.

The secret of this lump that Phil and I shared had caused me much distress during the previous two weeks; however, Phil insisted that we tell no one. My mother however, knowing her daughter, knew that something was not right with me during this time but did not push me for an answer when she approached me about my somber moods. Oh how much I wanted to share my concern with her, but I could not, as I had sworn to Phil that mom and dad were not to know. We were not to cause them any concern. I however could not help myself and had told three girlfriends during these two weeks, simply to release the pressure that was upon me and eventually he too had told a close friend.

On the day of his birthday, my concern was that it was five days later, and we still had not heard the result of this biopsy. Phil, however, was still not concerned. Earlier that day Phil and I had spoken on the phone, and when I asked him if he had heard from the doctor yet, he said to me. "No and I am not worried either Tanya. God is not going to give me sickness now. I have too much to do in this world." He did add that it was only a five percent concern for him. I was not convinced that all was well until we had heard the final result, and the simple fact that this result was taking so long was worrying me.

The day of Phil's birthday was long and arduous for me as each time the phone would ring my heart would pound as I wondered if this was the call we were waiting for. How I got through this day was by means of a fantasy that I had created and which replayed in my head constantly.

My fantasy was that we would be having dinner with mom and dad, one of her fabulous feasts. Phil would receive a phone call from his doctor whilst we were dining saying that all was well, that the lump was simply an infection of some sort and there was nothing to be concerned about. We would then tell mom and dad what we had been going through over the past two weeks and that everything was fine, and within days we could now move ahead and enjoy our dream holiday of a Caribbean cruise, on which we were due to leave three days later. We could then proceed to really celebrate Phil's birthday and enjoy the remainder of the evening.

This was my fantasy and what I needed to hold onto in order to get through this day, November 8, as the alternative was too unbearable to invest any more energy into. Anyway, that sort of thing would never happen to me and was not part of my life plan.

Intuitively I knew that Phil would receive the call whilst we were there for dinner. However, I did not know which way the pendulum would swing for us—after all it was a fifty-fifty chance either way. What kept me positive and thinking that the outcome would be favorable was simply the belief that surely Phil and I would never be given such an enormous hurdle to overcome in our lives. We were the perfect couple, with the perfect love and perfect life. This alone kept me positive and any other outcome would simply be a tragedy.

There still existed many facts that continued to fuel my fear. Firstly and most importantly, the lump was still there, and it was not getting any smaller. Secondly and my most fearful was what my intuition kept telling me, that Phil had cancer.

I could not rest and be at peace during this wait. Little snippets of peace would blanket me, but would be short lived as the fear would roll in over and pull the comfort of this blanket away from me as if taken by a corner and whisked away, often leaving me shivering.

That evening I was unable to enjoy mom's famous roast chicken, which as always, had a crunchy golden roasted skin, with the flavors of garlic, olive oil and salt in exactly the correct portions that only mom could measure to perfection.

It was just after 6.15 P.M. when Phil was about to cut his birthday cake when the sound of his cell phone ringing startled me. I recall the exact times very clearly as each moment was like an eternity for me that night. I knew that this was the call. My fantasy had begun. How would the pendulum swing?

Immediately my heart began to race as I heard Phil say, "Hello Rhona," he stood up from the dining room table and walked about ten feet to the kitchen bench with the cell phone in his left hand. I followed him staring at his face, his blue eyes, just to get some indication from his expressions, his words or his tone that all was well and I could then continue to live out my fantasy that I had so perfectly composed with my perfect outcome.

It was Phil's reply to Rhona in four words that altered my life forever, "What time tomorrow morning" that I knew the pendulum had not swung in our favor. I placed my hands on the kitchen bench, bent my head down and looked to the fawn tiled floor. The feeling of overwhelming nausea immediately came over me, and my breathing became heavy. It felt as though pins were jabbing into my head. I looked up and was facing Phil as he used his spare hand to look for a pen and began shuffling on the kitchen bench to look for some paper. He settled for the back of an envelope. He said very little at first then commenced to ask Rhona what the results were. She did not want to say on the phone, but he insisted that she tell him and said that he would rather know now than wait until the morning.

The walls of the kitchen began to turn around me as I watched Phil write on the back of this envelope the words, *lymphoma* and *small cell carcinoma* with a question mark. He ended his conversation to Rhona saying that he would see her at eight thirty the following morning.

Phil slowly placed his cell phone on top of the envelope that now held his fate, and I immediately draped my arms around his neck, terrified. I could not cry; I could barely get air into my lungs. I just held him as my head was nestled to his left. Phil appeared to be strong, in fact, like someone who did not want to be fussed over at that moment. He appeared in shock and was later to tell me that this was one time that he was in fact very frightened.

Meanwhile, my parents were still sitting at the dining room table confused and looking at us both. but by this stage knowing that something was seriously wrong. I can still see my mother's look of confusion as she kept saying to me, "Tanya, what is wrong?"

It was I who looked at my mother and said, "Mom, Phil has cancer." I recall seeing her look of confusion become a state of absolute disbelief in the words she had just heard. Briefly and hurriedly I informed them of the sequence of events during the previous two weeks.

Phil said very little, as he sat there, obviously in shock and stunned. It was then that my very intuitive mother told me that she had sensed something was wrong with me over the past weeks, that I was not the same. I was quiet and distant, but she was unable to pinpoint what was happening to me. However, she admitted that even this mother would never have expected something like this to be troubling her daughter, whom she knew so well.

Horror now replaced the joy that my parents had felt only ten minutes earlier as they were about to sing happy birthday to their son-in-law, who they referred to as their fourth son. "Not our Philip" were the words that mom repeated, I can still hear them.

Phil and I sat down again at the dining room table where his uncut birthday cake still remained. I wrapped my arms around my waist and started to cry in disbelief, rocking forwards and backwards in my chair. This cannot be happening to us; this is not true, not Phil, not my precious Phil, were the thoughts that were racing through my very confused mind.

Once again the dining room felt as though it was spinning around me, and all I wanted to do was to escape and return back two weeks to that feeling of bliss that I was experiencing in my perfect life.

Phil was slightly annoyed at my reaction, and he was trying to indicate to me that it was not something to panic about and not to frighten mom and dad any more than they should be. Mom and Dad both kept reassuring me of the same, saying that Phil would be fine and that I should calm down and that once they simply cut out the cancerous growth, "he will be fine," they kept saying.

Never in my life had I hoped that my parents would be right as they tried to comfort their little girl, their terrified little girl. Phil did not show his fear that night as I did; whilst he was in shock and frightened, he tried to be strong for us all.

No matter what anyone said to me at the dinner table that night, I had a terrible feeling. Something inside me knew that it would not be as simple as cutting out a cancerous lump. It was far greater than this, and something big was about to happen in our lives.

Phil's frame of mind changed to being slightly jovial, and he was determined to have a piece of his birthday cake that mum made for her son-in-law: banana with chocolate icing on top. He proceeded to cut his cake but without the usual joyous singing and ate this piece of cake in a manner to show his mum he appreciated and enjoyed the cake that she made for him. This was what he portrayed. Phil's state of happiness was in fact his own defense mechanism kicking in as he was trying to protect himself from what his consciousness at that moment was actually not able to assimilate. I believe that Phil also wanted to protect us from seeing what he was really feeling at that moment.

Whilst we were still at my parent's home that night, I went into the bathroom upstairs and made a phone call to my close friend Catherine. I was trying to speak as quietly as I could to tell her what we had just heard, and all I can remember is Catherine replying in her gentle Scottish accent saying "Oh no."

Catherine had been my main support, not only during the previous two weeks, but also during many other painful journeys in my life. It was Catherine whom I had phoned in the early hours of a cold May morning in 1998 after we had discovered that my father had just been diagnosed with cancer. We cried together on the phone that morning and we would be shedding many more tears together in the months to follow this phone call.

As we drove away from mom and dad's, I recall them standing at the front door of their home saying goodbye with hand waves that were not like the usual ones of joy but simply raising their hands in some form of acknowledgement, neither of us really knowing of what.

I knew very well what would happen behind that closed front door once they went inside. In spite of being strong for both Phil and I that night, normally mom and dad do not mind expressing their feelings, and this would have been done whilst they were together behind that closed door. Their tears would have flowed as they held each other, in utter disbelief of what they had just learned, of what had just been asked of their little girl and her husband to now endure in their life.

On our way home, not a lot was spoken in the car between Phil and I; we were silent. However we wanted to commence our fight against this beast inside Phil's body immediately. Phil was an Area Manager for a supermarket chain, and his office was at our local supermarket, only a five minute drive from our home. Phil had always kept a very healthy diet and was at one point in his life a vegetarian, so he was very knowledgeable about food groups and what his body needed.

We had decided to stop there before returning home and we began buying organic vegetables, fruits, cereals, vitamins, and anything that we felt would help cleanse Phil's body and somehow take away this nightmare. We were in shock and disbelief as we frantically looked around the market, wanting to find anything that would assist us and provide us with a feeling that we were doing something towards the cause.

Later that evening, the two of us sat in the lounge together praying that somehow this nightmare for us would end, and we could return to our simple life as it was only two weeks earlier.

All we knew was that Phil had either Lymphoma or Small Cell Carcinoma; we knew nothing about either of these types of cancer. I had heard that Lymphoma was treatable and knew of people whom had survived this type of cancer but was not sure about those other three words. Somehow, with the word *small* in the description, Phil naively assumed that Small Cell Carcinoma was perhaps not that bad. Little did we know how deadly three words could be.

We were later to learn that small cell carcinoma of unknown primary (SCUP) is a deadly and uncommon cancer that is usually diagnosed in the lymph nodes, liver, brain or bone. The prognosis varies from a few months to several years depending on the location, extent of disease and response to therapy.

The following morning I was physically and emotionally shattered. Apart from momentarily dozing, neither of us slept that night. Phil got up and went to the gym early that day, as he did every other morning. Today would be no different for him. He was going to continue with his life. I did not have the energy to do much at all; my body was in shock and shaking. It astounded me that Phil actually got up and did his usual gym routine.

At five thirty that morning I phoned my friends, Sue and Meg, the other two friends who were aware of our dilemma during the previous weeks, and I just wept. Whatever sleep I got the night before was not enough to remove the nightmare when I awoke that morning. Yes, last night did happen and yes, my fantasy that I had so perfectly scripted did not come true.

When Phil returned from his workout, he told me that his friend Tony stopped him at the gym and said "Mate, you are looking really good, what are you doing? I have never seen you look in better shape." Phil told me that he sarcastically wanted to say, "oh just get cancer mate, that's how you do it."

Phil and I went together for the eight–thirty appointment. Even though we were early, Phil's doctor Rhona came out to get us as soon as we arrived. The first thing I noticed as she approached us was firstly her gentle but very nervous smile and then her beautiful bush of black wavy hair.

Rhona had been wonderful to us both in the past. I had always respected her for how thorough she was and her beautiful manner during the times when I sat with her and cried to her about not being able to conceive and become pregnant. She was originally from South Africa, and I often felt comforted by her accent and soft voice. However, on this morning, no matter how softly and calmly Rhona spoke, when I heard the words "secondary cancer," it was as if she was shouting them directly into my face.

My knowledge of cancer was reasonable, and what I did know for sure was that secondary cancer was not good and it meant that there was a primary cancer elsewhere in Phil's body. The biopsy result was not yet conclusive, and further tests were being performed to rule out lymphoma. They believed that Phil had small cell carcinoma, which we were told apparently often originates in the lung. This meant that whatever was in his lymph nodes in his armpit was not all there was, and it was not going to be a matter of simply "cutting out a lump."

Once again I began to feel nauseated, and the room was closing in on me. I could barely look at Phil, who was also in shock and feeling the same disbelief that I was. Immediately I visualized a tumor inside Phil, sitting on his lung. Then I began to tremble harder and stronger, wanting to escape from this cage that I was placed in. All I wanted was to return to my life before October 25 when all was well in my world, and I was ignorant of what in fact lay ahead in my life.

This was November 9. We were due to go on a Caribbean Cruise only two days later—a holiday that Phil desperately needed and one that up until October 25 I had looked forward to so much.

My immediate reaction was that we could not go on this holiday and that Phil had to begin treatment of some sort to remove this cancer from his body immediately. Rhona already had a verbal suggestion from an oncologist that Phil was not to travel, and I agreed. "We cannot go, please, let's stay home and get you well. Start treatment, do whatever to stop this beast." Phil said no, and he insisted that we go on this holiday. For him this was to be the beginning of his healing. He said he was tired and needed to rest and was adamant in Rhona's office that nothing or no one would hold him back from this holiday which he so desperately needed.

He became angry with me in the office at my fearful reaction. I did not want to lose another moment to this disease which was inside Phil's body and what I sensed was moving rapidly.

It is only as I now write this that I can look back and feel, Phil, you followed your heart Your intuition and your decision was perfect. Who was I to suggest what you were to do with your body? Phil said no to everything that everyone was firing at him that morning. "This is my decision and I need to do this, we will go on this holiday, I need this holiday, I need this rest, I want to start my healing by resting my body, and I will not have chemotherapy." It was as simple as that for Phil; this was his body and his call.

I don't know how we got home that morning. All we had to do was to walk two hundred meters from the Doctor's surgery which was across the road and down a side street from our home. We walked in silence. Looking at Phil was my greatest pain. At that moment, I could see his fear as we crossed the busy road, both of us oblivious to all the traffic on that Tuesday morning. Tuesdays would not be the same for me for many a month after that day.

Once we arrived home we made a couple of phone calls: one to Phil's friend and confidante Debbie and once again I saw his fear. I held him tightly with my arms around his waist as he spoke to her.

A few moments later, I called mom and dad and told them in my Croatian tongue that it was worse than we thought—that it was on Phil's lungs and who knows where else. I recall having to repeat it to Dad so that he understood and even louder again so he could hear what I was saying. This however was disrupted by the wailing in the background that came from my mother's heart. I cried as I told my father. I could hear his tears also and feel his heart being taken from his chest as I did my best to explain what I understood of Phil's condition.

I made this call from our bedroom as I was looking out at nothing on the street. It was a busy main road with the constant sound of cars going past. This morning however, the sound of the cars did not register in my thinking and the noise that would so often have bothered me just did not compute, because all I knew and could think about was that my husband Phil had cancer. Nothing else mattered any more.

Phil asked that my parents tell no one of his diagnosis, not even my brothers. I pleaded with him that we not keep this a secret that my parents needed support here also, and he finally agreed that yes my brothers could know, but no one else was to know at this point. My father left mom alone for awhile as he went to my brother Zel's office to tell him what was now happening in our family.

Phil headed off to work shortly after our phone calls, and, once he had departed, Zel phoned me, and finally I was able to release the anguish that had lodged itself in my chest that morning. We were both in tears as we gently spoke. I was sitting on the edge of my bed, facing the mirror of my bedroom suite looking unbelievably at a distressed woman in the reflection as if I was watching a movie. I could not believe and did not want to believe that it was actually I who was looking back at me.

Horror overcame me as I watched this movie, and I began crying to Zel that I did not want to lose Phil. I did not want him to die. Once again, my arm was wrapped around my stomach as I sat on the edge of my bed rocking forwards and backwards. Did I think that this cradling of self would ease my pain, perhaps? I will never forget the words that Zel then spoke to me, "Tanya, if it is God's will to take our brother Phil, then one thing I know is that he will be in Heaven, and that is what really matters." Whilst I knew this to be true, this was not to be the outcome; it could not be.

Phil did want to visit his sister Marie that morning to let her know what had happened to us over the past two weeks and what he was now facing. Marie was special to him, very similar to his mother, Moira, who had already passed away some 18 years earlier. Marie was his "big" sister, with a big heart, who had a huge love for her "big baby" brother.

When we arrived at her shop she knew that something was wrong, since we had both shown up unannounced—something that had never occurred before. As I walked towards her I could see her apprehension which was hidden behind a smile that was placed on her face as if it was painted on.

It was Phil who began to tell her that he had cancer and the brief details of what we knew, and then came his first tears. Finally he was able to let his tears come with his big sister. He did not need to be brave at this moment. How he would have loved to have had his mom with him at that time I am sure.

Marie was stoic. The three of us held each other closely in her shop as I then completed the story which Phil had begun, as much as I could, with the only words that I knew, "cancer, secondary, probably lung." I was strong, but my voice was trembling. I too wanted to cry, but I could not. This was Phil's time now to shed those much needed tears, and, as difficult as it was for me at this time, I held mine in for now.

Those other big words, *small cell carcinoma,* meant nothing to me at this point. In time however, they would haunt me—they would wake me in the night and it would be a long time before I could see or hear those words without trembling.

The three of us continued to hold each other and formed a little triangle, me, hoping that these cuddles and love would be what would start to shrink this foreign beast that had lodged itself inside Phil's beautiful body.

Phil was such a proud man. He trained hard at the gym and always liked to look his best. He was well known for his beautiful wardrobe of clothes. He was naturally lean. At six foot three inches tall he weighed in at only eighty four kilograms when we met; as he did a lot of running. However, that was something I knew would change after being in a Croatian family. He needed some padding; my mom thought, and she had much joy in doing this!

By the time of our wedding day some two years later, Phil was ninety kilograms and at the time of his diagnosis he was ninety six kilograms, of which he was very proud. I remember one night when he was coming to bed as he proudly waltzed in to our room after his typical lengthy shower, and I said to him, "Do you love your body honey"?

"Hell yeah," was his jovial reply, "it's the only one God gave me and I am going to look after it!" This was something Phil always did.

No matter what shape or size we naturally are, I realized first hand at the time of Phil's illness how lucky we were that we had healthy bodies.

TWO

The Diagnosis

This journey started for us during the final weekend of October 2004. It was the Monday of Labor weekend. Phil and I lived in Jervois Road, New Zealand, and, like so many New Zealanders, we spent the day in the garden at our home, weeding and planting our summer vegetables. It was a beautiful hot day. Phil had his shirt off and, we had the music going. I remember it well. Phil was playing a CD continuously that weekend which had the theme of not giving up.

Our three cats, Chi, Rudi and Fergus, would have been with us that day, either sheltering in the trees, or amongst the tomato plants as Fergus often did. Being a grey tabby, he blended in rather well with the garden dirt and was the first to leap out at the sight or sound of a tweet from a bird.

We both loved our garden at this home; it was in fact our favourite part of the property. The house was a 1930s bungalow with three large bedrooms and a very large lounge area with an oval alcove and, above the seats in the alcove, beautiful stained glass windows. We had many a gathering in the very large lounge.

Apart from the bedrooms, the house had beautiful polished wooden rimu floors. I would love to say that they were always shiny, but they were forever covered in cat prints and muddy skid marks where the cats would sprint in from the outside garden, chasing one another, and slide on the polished floors when turning a corner trying to outrun one another. The humour that this created for us was worth having the muddy floors.

Our home was on a main road which was not ideal due to the road noise being a constant source of frustration for us. Our pride and joy was the back garden which had a beautiful indoor/outdoor flow with the dining area. This was one area of the house which we had developed ourselves. Looking out from the kitchen and dining area past a covered deck with colonial drops to the left was the vegetable garden, which I took so much pride in. To the right was a very full palm garden which had many shades of green through it. In between these two was a centre garden with rows of tomatoes and capsicum. Dad taught us all we knew about maintaining the garden and how to grow the vegetables. In fact, he often kept an eye on it, and Phil and I would often fall into a mild panic if dad announced that he was coming over. "Oh no, the auditor is coming; how does the garden look?" We would laugh.

This Monday was a particularly lovely hot spring day; in fact, the entire weekend was, and I felt especially happy that weekend. Phil and I would always feel excitement in the spring. As the mornings began to get lighter and the days longer. We would awaken early to head off to the gym or whatever exercise we were doing that morning and leave the rest of the day to do other things for the weekend. On that particular weekend, for some reason Phil did not go to the gym which I found unusual. I would later learn why not.

I felt joy that entire weekend. In fact, the day before on the Sunday afternoon I wrote in my journal, "Today God, I am here to give thanks to You for my wonderful life. I do feel blessed. I feel as though You have given me so much in my life with Phil. He is such a wonderful man." Once again I wrote about our desire to have a child of our own and my final sentence about this was once again "whatever Your will be Lord." I did not know when writing these words at that time how they would become one of my greatest prayers for the rest of my life.

On the following day, that hot spring Monday, once again I gave thanks for my life. It was about four o'clock by the time I'd had enough in the garden and returned into the house to start washing the freshly picked lettuce. Whilst in the kitchen looking at Phil still in the garden I reflected to myself that I had never been this happy in my life. Instantly as these thoughts and feelings of joy came to me, a small voice in my head responded to me by saying, *yes but for how long will it last?* I dismissed them. I knew that they were old messages that I carried with me—that one should not experience joy for too long, because it never really lasted.

That evening we were sitting in our lounge, Phil on a chair to my left and me, on the couch with my legs nestled underneath me, often our usual seats. All was silent until all of a sudden Phil announced to me, "Tarn, I think I need to see a doctor." I was alarmed as he did not like doctors or dentists and did everything to avoid them.

"Why"? I replied.

"I have got a lump under my arm," he said in a very sheepish, almost childlike way.

I remember freezing at that point, "Since when"? I asked,

"Oh, it has been here for about six or eight weeks," he said and at that point felt very uncomfortable that he had not mentioned it to me before then.

My response was one of slight agitation, however I kept my voice to a level where it did not show, and my words were "oh Phil," but what I was really saying was, why did you not tell me sooner? I could see Phil's discomfort or nervousness as he was telling me as this would have been the response that he expected from me.

He showed me the lump, and I was petrified with what I saw. This lump was large, and what frightened me more was that after two months it was still there. I did my best not to express my alarm when I saw this lump, however, quietly as I was looking and touching it, we both knew that this was not normal.

Time stood still for me at that moment. My body went into some form of shock, and it felt as though I was beginning to freeze over. The room began to spin, and I so desperately did not want Phil to see my fear but that was what it was—something inside me felt very scared.

That night when Phil was not in my presence I secretly found one of my health books and looked up lymphoma cancer or cancers of the lymph nodes and Hodgkin's disease. Looking under symptoms I attempted to stay calm and not panic as he did not have any of the other apparent symptoms, no night sweats, no weight loss, and no other lumps. I was however, still petrified.

That night we hopped into bed and prayed together. Phil asked that we pray for his good health. Of course this would be what we prayed for I thought. Neither of us slept well that night, and the fear I grew to know so well had enveloped my being and no logic could ease these feelings that night for me.

We went to the doctors the following morning, and, whilst doing an examination of Phil's naked chest, Rhona pointed out to us more swelling around the area of his collar bone and left breast. She turned to look at me and asked if I too did see it. I was able to acknowledge that yes I did see it then, even though I had not noticed it before. Phil was looking at me at the time awaiting my response. All I wanted to say was no, I don't see anything; you are imagining it Rhona, but I could not lie to myself or to Phil.

Rhona sent Phil for a blood test at the laboratory across the road from the doctor's rooms, and, whilst we were there in the waiting room, I saw her coming with another form in her hand. This frightened me, especially when I saw that it was a request for a chest X-ray, "preferably as soon as possible" she quietly said.

Knowing how thorough Rhona is I sensed that she was concerned also. The results from the chest x-ray and blood tests over the next few days came back normal, and we were ecstatic to hear this news. If Phil had cancer, then surely it would have shown up in the blood. He was going to be fine, and we would go on our cruise very happy people.

The next few days appeared to be normal. However, for me there was still a slight concern, which I just kept to myself. I did not feel that this concern would leave me until a biopsy of the lump was performed, and they told us conclusively that Phil was fine, and this lump was simply some form of fatty tissue or infection.

Only a few nights later, on Saturday October 30 I did begin to worry. *Something* in me had altered and I went to bed feeling very low and this unexplained darkness came over me. During the early hours of the next morning I awoke to fear. My fear was that somewhere deep inside I knew that Phil had cancer. What also awoke me was the heat that was being generated from his body. Was this a night sweat?

Whatever it was that caused the shift in my senses, I bolted upright in my bed, and I knew that Phil had cancer. I did not tell Phil that I awoke during the night, and the following morning I was brought to uncontrollable tears when my cat Fergus scratched me. I just could not remove from my mind the thoughts that Phil had cancer, and what frightened me more was that so often my intuition was right.

Phil often commented about my intuition and that I needed to follow it more and asked me a few times that morning what was wrong. I sensed that he suspected my tears were not about the cat scratch but about something deeper.

Soon after I took myself out for a walk in the morning sunshine and released the rest of my tears and did my best to let this all go as I had guests coming over that afternoon that I had to be prepared for. Once again that afternoon, my mother asked me on a number of occasions what was bothering me. She knew her daughter.

The following day, Monday November 1, was another beautiful sunny day. In spite of not having a diagnosis, inside, my heart was pure dread. Somewhere buried inside I knew that Phil was going to die. I spent much of this day in tears as I walked in the beautiful sunshine along the marina, under the Auckland Harbor Bridge with my sunglasses on hiding the tears as they streamed down my face.

As I walked I listened to a new CD I had purchased and one song particularly made me cry as I imagined what Phil's funeral would be like. This would be a beautiful song to play at his funeral I thought. The words touched me as they symbolized how I felt that my life had changed since I had been with Phil. He encouraged me on my journey to be me and to really start discovering the true potential within me. Phil encouraged me to rise up and be more than I could be. He felt secure enough in himself to walk beside me during this process. In spite of his continued encouragement I would still often reprieve into the safety of my nest so as to not really experience myself at my full potential.

The following day, Tuesday, I had decided that this was all very silly, that Phil would be fine and that my tears were uncalled for; I was once again happy. Still a question lingered for me, which was, why is the lump still there and why is it not getting smaller?

As I lay one night in the darkness I observed Phil as he was getting out of bed. I could see his silhouette as he raised himself from the bed. The first thing he did was with reach underneath his left armpit to feel for any change. I pretended to be asleep and did not mention this to Phil; it did however suggest to me that he too was asking himself the same question about this lump, why was it still there.

It was not until the following Thursday, November 3, that Phil was having a biopsy. I seem to always remember the weather on these significant days, and once again the skies were brilliant blue as we drove out to the laboratory together. This gentle young Indian man who performed the procedure informed us that they were not fatty deposits and he made some comment about *lymph tissue*. Phil did ask him if he had seen this before, to which the young man replied that yes he had but could not comment until they performed the biopsy so as not to give false information.

Phil took this as a positive sign. I did not like it at all. I was still fearful and wanted these lumps to be fatty deposits. Also, I did not think that it was a good sign when the young man said that the results would take up to five days.

As we drove away from the laboratory I asked Phil if we could tell my parents. To date still no one knew, only the three of my girlfriends whom I needed to share this with. Phil immediately said no and that there was no point in worrying anyone and that we would tell them when it was over and say that it was all a false alarm. I attempted to argue the point that my reasoning for telling them was to have more people providing us with support. This was what I felt we needed. It was what *I knew I needed*. The load was already too heavy for me to carry, but his reply was a definite no.

Two days later on November 6, Saturday night, we went to five o'clock Mass as normal, and we headed out to dinner to an Italian restaurant with Phil's sister Marie and her husband, Neil, to have an early celebration of Phil's birthday. My recollection of Mass that night was my prayer. I felt deeply in my heart that no matter what the diagnosis was, everything would be alright. This brought a tinge of joy to me. I truly felt that Phil would survive this. Whatever happened, he would be our miracle.

That night at dinner Phil thoroughly enjoyed himself. Nowhere in his being, well, only five percent he said, was he even remotely thinking that anything would be wrong with him. "Why would God bring sickness upon me Tarn? I have got too much work to do on this earth. He won't have me be sick."

I could not help myself as I watched him that night painting on a smile for Marie and Neil but still wondering what the next few days would bring. I remember even wondering if what he ordered for dinner was something healthy enough for his *condition*. I could not erase the fear that was lodged at the deepest level for me.

As the days passed and the longer it took for the diagnosis to return, the more concerned I felt, and somehow I knew that the call would come at my parent's place on the night of his birthday, as it did.

The days following the news on November 8 were nothing short of pure horror, and for me they were in fact in some way the worst of them all during this entire journey. When not in Phil's presence I cried constantly. I was in shock; my body was shaking and burning energy rapidly. Phil wanted very few people to know, and the day following only a handful of people were told: my brothers, Marie and Neil, Lois and Allan, and Phil's friend Debbie.

After the appointment with Rhona on the morning of November 9, she managed to get Phil an appointment with an oncologist late that afternoon to discuss the possibility of Phil traveling. Rhona had already spoken to the oncologist of Phil's stubborn streak and the importance of this holiday for him. She had witnessed this that morning in her office.

I had phoned my own counselor David that morning and told him what had happened and that I did not want to go on this holiday and his words to me, very firmly I might add were that "This was Phil's life, and he had to live his life the way he wanted to." I surrendered to those words.

That night, the oncologist gave Phil permission to travel on our holiday however once we returned more tests would be required which would be immediately followed by treatment.

Phil was determined to go on this holiday and wasn't very interested in any treatments. He already had told Rhona that morning what they could all do with the chemotherapy, and a holiday was what he needed. Personally, I just wanted to stay home in the comfort of my family, my home, my cats, everything that was safe for me and to proceed in getting

Phil fixed. I wanted to get this beast out of his body and to commence doing so immediately.

After our appointment with the oncologist, I did get a glimmer of hope that perhaps things were not that bad and that at least we can go away and forget about things and deal with it upon our return. At that moment it felt as though we could both run away to the Caribbean and leave everything, including this cancer, behind. Was this another sign that Phil would actually get through this?

That night my parents came over, mom delivering food as she always did, as did Marie and Neil. Somehow, having those you love close to you is one thing that makes the pain appear less intense. It is as if they carry some of that pain for you, and of course you want them to constantly reassure you that all in your world would be well again. That night I felt like this helpless little girl needing my mom and dad to tell me that everything was going to be alright for me.

The following day on Wednesday my friend Sue came over. She and my mother were with me during the day. I could not be alone. Phil once again arose at five-thirty and went to the gym then headed off for work. I am not really sure what had registered for him at that time. Perhaps if he just kept going, all this might all go away? He was looking forward to this holiday, and getting away seemed to be his main focus.

My memories of that Wednesday were dark, of being in the shower, in shock, disbelief, pain, horror, unbearable tears, waling, standing there and letting the water fall over me as I cried to God and for the first time asked Him Why? I remember thinking that my life, our life, as we knew it, would never be the same again.

"Why God, why us, we have always been so faithful to You. Why did the pendulum not swing favorably for us?" Sue told me that she was not going to cry in front of me, that she would be strong for me that day; however, nothing could have stopped us from holding each other and crying together that morning in my office.

Sue and I had been friends for eighteen years. She was once my beauty therapist, and on that Wednesday as a treat for me, she laid me on the couch and tinted my eyelashes so that somehow I could lie for a few moments to relax and have pretty eyes for my trip away the following day.

As I lay on the couch that day, a warm spring day, I asked that a blanket be placed over my body as the shock swept through me and the cold covered my shaking body. It was an unbearable day for me, and I remember my mother constantly telling me that "I was not to do this to myself, that I too would become sick, that I had to somehow calm myself," if only I could have. However, nothing could have alleviated my pain that day apart from awaking to what was in fact only a bad dream.

This was the final night at home before we were to leave for the cruise, and my dear friend Catherine was once again coming over to house sit and, most importantly, cat sit. Having three cats made it somewhat difficult to go away, and I would not even entertain for a moment the thought of putting them in a cattery.

Catherine, Phil and I stayed up and chatted, and it was the first time since Phil's diagnosis that I heard him share his deep feelings. Perhaps having Catherine there allowed him to share more as he would not feel that he was burdening me totally with his concerns. I heard his words. I heard his feelings. In a soft-spoken tone, both Catherine and I heard what was in his heart.

My own heart bled for Phil as I watched him and listened. All I wanted to do was to embrace him and remove his pain, to take that pain on myself, but I could not.

The scene was similar to and reminded me of how I felt over six years earlier when my father was diagnosed with cancer. I was sitting at his dining room table with him not long after his diagnosis, crying, saying to him, "I wished that it was me that had the cancer, it would be easier for me to carry this than to watch your pain." I truly wished that it was me that was ill, as this somehow would have been easier for me to take than to watch someone I loved suffer.

Here I was, once again, this Wednesday night wishing that it was me having to go through this journey. Such a scenario would have been far less painful than to watch my beautiful Phil suffer this way.

THREE

The Cruise

The following day we were due to leave for the Cruise, and again Phil went to the gym for his early morning workout as if nothing had changed in his life.

Catherine and I left for a long walk that morning from the home Phil and I shared in Herne Bay. The days were longer, and the sun arose earlier, so it was already light. I felt stronger during our walk. My tears at this point had dried up, and my body had somewhat settled down although it still felt as though I was surviving on pure adrenalin. My manner and conversation on this walk was very matter of fact—this would happen; that would happen, and this was how I would live my life from now on.

As we were about to walk under the Auckland Harbor Bridge with the morning sun beaming through its railings I said to Catherine, "I will never marry again nor will I ever be involved with anyone ever again." To which she calmly replied, "Will you not Tanya?" My words were bizarre. I was in shock and angry that this was now happening in my life, and what I was really saying was, "God, I am angry at You, and I will never put myself into a situation that could possibly cause me any form of pain like this ever again."

I talked continuously on this walk. My words seemed so clinical, and dear Catherine, no matter how insane I may have sounded that morning to anyone else who would have been there, allowed me to let it all out. She would have known for sure what was happening for me at that time when clearly I did not.

Later that morning my parents came over with lunch, and Zel also came over. Having family over and the busyness that this created took our minds off things and even created some laughter. Zel in his usual diplomatic way said, "Hey Phil, let me see your lump." Of course Phil took off his shirt and displayed the lump that he up until this time kept to himself.

During the conversation Phil also told Zel then that under no circumstance would he do chemotherapy, to which Zel responded in his legal manner, "Well, the jury is not out on that yet Phil, and as your legal representative I will have to have an opinion on that." Zel made this comment with some nervous laughter attached and may have been joking on some level, however I knew that Phil was not.

In spite of the stress that we had endured during the past three days we both felt excitement at going away, as if leaving the country was in some way leaving behind the reality of our situation. I had changed my thinking about going away, and it felt right for us to get away together; I felt at peace that this was to be totally Phil's call, and I accepted his decision.

We were on a waiting list to fly business class to Los Angeles, and by coincidence we bumped into Phil's cousin who worked at the check-in area at the airport. Once again, we felt that we were taken care of, and yes we ended up in business class. No other person on that flight deserved it more than we did, I thought to myself. From Los Angeles we flew to Florida to board the cruise ship at Fort Lauderdale.

No matter what little bouts of excitement about our holiday would enter my heart during that twelve hour flight, unfortunately nothing could chisel away at the black boulder of horror that was also lodged in there. Whenever I would awaken during that flight, this darkness would circle around me, and I could not escape from it.

Being away on this cruise was bitter sweet. Phil had worked so hard during the year on two major projects and desperately needed the rest. It was to be a well deserved holiday of a lifetime for us and much needed time together, however what also accompanied us was this darkness that, no matter how much we tried to eliminate from our thoughts, was always by our side.

Phil and I prayed so much together whilst we were away, and soon others would be praying for us as we shared more of Phil's situation. Often the prayer would be that I be released of the fear that had taken over my entire being, as if everyone could see underneath my mask how crippled I was by this feeling. Many more would pray for that exact intention in the months to come, including me.

One night when we were alone and had finished praying together I felt a real peace in my heart which I interpreted that Phil would survive this ordeal, and I said to him, "Honey I no longer fear you dying." He misinterpreted my words and thought he heard me say that I no longer feared his impending death. Immediately I saw the fear in his eyes as he asked me to explain to him what I meant; did I know something that he did not? I explained to him that his interpretation was wrong and that this was not what I felt, not at that moment anyway.

I could see absolutely no reason why Phil would be removed from this earth when he was such a mentor to others, and his recovery from cancer would give such a message of hope to all those who were suffering from a similar fate. That evening I truly did not feel that Phil was going to die, and I was grateful for having an evening of reprieve from my fear.

My confidence was short lived as the following morning I awoke to fear which was now becoming my familiar friend; once again the reality of what was happening in our lives had struck me down. I could not shake this terrible darkness that hovered around me and my fears about the worst possible scenario, and what made it more difficult were my attempts to hide this fear from Phil. There was this false demeanor around me that I hoped Phil did not sense, however, he knew me so well I was probably only fooling myself.

As we sailed from Fort Lauderdale Phil was on the balcony of our cabin calling out to me, and he was so excited, "Tarn, come and have a look at this." He was genuinely happy, and, whilst I showed Phil an excitement which I hoped appeared real, inside my heart was breaking. On the balcony I draped my arms around his waist as he voiced his joy, and yes I agreed with him that this was the trip of our lifetime, whilst trying to hold onto his belief that it was the first of many more to come.

Phil was taking photos of everything possible as the boat sailed away.

This was where we were different, however, I allowed this difference just to be. That night I realized how unimportant it really was. I liked to have photos of people in them, Phil however took photos of everything—signs, run down properties, plants, anything in fact, simply so that when he looked back on these images they would remind him of his experiences and feelings at a certain point in time.

How grateful I now feel to have these images to look at and know the exact feelings I was experiencing and the feelings that Phil was sharing with me as he took them as we sailed away from Fort Lauderdale. More importantly it was Phil who took them and they were his choice of image at that time.

The following day would be Phil's darkest since his diagnosis and the first time that I would see him shed tears like I had not seen before during our entire ten years together. It was a day when we had the opportunity to connect with a doctor so that we could have a greater understanding on what Phil's diagnosis actually meant.

We both already had been given information about the severity of Phil's condition and the treatments available from our conversations in Auckland. There was however an opportunity for a second opinion, so we took it. Others were there asking questions. We waited to speak to him, and then I gently pushed myself through the crowd. The doctor could see that I had been there for some time and requested that I come forward which I did, however Phil remained in the background.

All I did was pass to him with my nervous hand the diagnostic report that we received back in Auckland, a report that I actually had great difficulty in handling as to me it felt like a written death sentence. By this time I had studied this page. I knew the report nearly word for word, and I could visualize exactly how it looked. There were words on this page that I had never seen before, and had to look up their meaning on the internet to somehow understand how they affected Phil.

This doctor was a big man with black rather wavy hair with an incredibly deep voice, like none I had ever heard before. He took this same page from my hand and with his other hand placed his glasses on and read for a moment. My heart beat ferociously as we waited for his opinion, just as it is now as I write these words.

I can recall so clearly how I felt at that time, the room, the people and Phil's quiet presence behind me as I took charge of these moments. This doctor removed his glasses with one hand and held Phil's fate in the other. His look was enough to warn me of what was about to be said. We both knew that the hope that we were desperate for was not to come from the words of this knowledgeable man, but we knew that what he said we must listen to.

His first words to us were, "Would you like me to speak to you privately about this?" to which Phil courageously replied from behind, "no." The doctor's next words were "I would recommend that you do both chemotherapy and radiotherapy as these lymphatic cancers can be very aggressive." At that point I went into shock and don't quite recall what happened for the moments after hearing those words. His deep voice was now piercing me as he continued to speak, and all I wanted to do was to shout *stop, don't say any more!*

My next recollection was both Phil and I moving away from the crowd and this very pleasant woman coming up to us and telling Phil to be strong, to remove all stress from his life as her husband lost his battle to cancer which she felt was due to the excessive stress he carried. We thanked her but really did not want to hear her views or anyone else's views for that matter. We had heard enough and we both needed to escape from the suffocation that we were feeling at that time.

Our cabin was on the next floor up, so Phil and I together made our way up the wide staircase which was in the centre of the ship. Somehow we got there; in silence we walked. We got to the top of the stairs, and I began to walk ahead of Phil, leading the way for him knowing that he needed every bit of assistance to get to our cabin and soon. I opened the door to our cabin, and allowed Phil in and as soon as he stepped in he cried out allowed like I had never seen before. His tears and anguish stopped my own; there was no room for me to express what was building inside of me, and there it had to remain.

Phil wept loudly as he angrily cried out, "Why, why, I have never smoked, I have looked after my body, I have not hurt others, why, why?" Sitting beside him to his right I held him, both of my arms were around him as he continued to cry and wail, to finally allow his pain and fear to arise and be released from his being. Somehow I gathered strength at that moment, from where it came I do not know. All I knew was that this had to be Phil's time and my grief had to remain buried deeply inside for now.

As long as I breathe I will never forget his next words to me which were, "Tarn, I do not want to leave you a widow." This was the first time I heard Phil voice that his death was now a possibility to him; this could be the final outcome to this journey. Hearing this was devastating and frightening for me as Phil had such a wisdom that I often took his word as gospel. Please Phil, don't say this; I don't want to hear it, were my thoughts.

This scene was agony for me. Phil, my rock, was falling apart in front of me. My poor darling Phil was falling apart. How would I cope; I cannot carry this load; please Lord, carry us both at this time, were my pleas.

This day was particularly rough at sea, and the boat swayed slightly all day. That evening it became considerably worse, and being one who would often have motion sickness, by this stage of the evening I was feeling rather unwell. Phil had released his tears and, at a time when he so needed me, I lay on the bed. By this stage I was rather nauseous. I could not say what caused it the most—the rough seas of the present moment or my fears or the rough future that lay ahead for us. Whatever it was I could not get up off the bed for fear that I would be ill.

Once Phil felt that he was strong enough to leave the room—we decided to go to the main restaurant for dinner. Phil was hungry and I needed something in my empty stomach to settle it somehow. Both of us, particularly Phil, went from a state of absolute unbearable pain into a euphoric state of shock. It was as though he was on a high as if the past two hours had not happened for him.

All I could do was to slip some ice cream into my queasy stomach; Phil however indulged in the smorgasbord as I had not seen him do for days. He ate everything available to him, including an enormous dessert. His mood seemed rather unusual, and I did feel at the time that he had entered a state of shock. On some level I was relieved that he was having a few hours of reprieve from his agony that had struck him only hours before. I don't remember our conversation during dinner, only two things—how much he was enjoying his food and thinking that if we act happy then perhaps this nightmare might leave us, and we will not actually be experiencing what is really happening in our lives.

Soon my body could not take any more of the movement of the ship, and the remainder of our evening out was me needing to leave the restaurant to go to the toilets to be ill and release the tears that had built up during the previous hours. My body again began to shake with fear and my stomach was churning from the constant movement of the ship, so I remained outside in the cool air. Phil soon joined me still rather jovial and feeling rather satisfied with his feed, as he would call it!

We made our way back to the cabin and lay in bed and prayed. All we knew to do was pray. To whom else would we turn to if not our God? We had convinced ourselves that this trial was sent for a reason, that Phil would survive and tell his story to many and give others strength and hope who were also coping with such a journey. This was what we chose to believe at that time as any other reason just did not make sense to us.

The next few days our voyage took us to beautiful destinations, Jamaica and the Bahamas to name a few. We did our best to enjoy our time together—to live as if Phil was going to survive and death was not an option. We removed it from our thoughts during this time. We enjoyed the most wonderful day in the Bahamas; we walked, swam in the surf and shopped as if there were no cares in our life. We enjoyed the present moment, and I believe that we were both able to remove the dread in our lives at this time. Phil of course took photos, of everything!

Together we sat on the beach in the Bahamas. I sat behind Phil and caressed his back, deep in thought with no words spoken, simply enjoying the moment. Phil loved to swim and could not wait to get into the surf. I watched as this beautiful man walked into the surf and threw himself into the waves as if he did not have a care in the world. I watched in amazement at how strong his body looked, and I wondered how was it that such a healthy looking body was slowly being attacked inside by this foreigner. As he freely splashed his way through the surf he would often look up at the beach with his beaming smile. I responded with an equally joyous smile and wondered what was really going on for him, what was really buried under that smile of his.

Everyone was actually rather baffled that Phil looked so well at this time considering that he had advanced secondary cancer with a diagnosis that often brought about weight loss as one of the initial symptoms. He looked strong and one would never have known as his weight was stable.

That day as we were leaving the beach at the Bahamas we bought matching crosses from the local girls on the side of the road. They were made from a special dark stone which we were told was a healing stone. Perhaps it was a sales pitch. We did not know nor did I care. This was a sign; yes, it must be we thought. Phil would live as we looked for any signs.

A few days after our return back to Auckland however Phil's cross one day mysteriously had broken in half. This frightened me as only a few days prior to this something else had occurred which also alarmed me.

Just before our wedding day we purchased a set of rosary beads called a marriage rosary. Instead of the usual large loop of five decades there were in fact two loops, ten decades—one loop for each person which met at the centre and were joined with the small string of beads which led to the cross on the end.

When we returned home we found one string of these beads mysteriously broken; in fact, one entire loop was broken in half. This occurrence alone sent me into a spin, however when Phil's cross was also found broken I then became fearful. Not only was I looking for any positive signs, but I also became hypersensitive to the negative and wondered what it all meant, if anything.

We were moving between the various stages of grief at this point, denial that this was happening in our lives and choosing not to accept any scenario but recovery, to bargaining with God and willing to do anything for a miracle and then back into the comfort of denial again. If only You would heal Phil, we will dedicate our entire lives to Your will for us Lord, were our thoughts and prayers.

The denial was a coping mechanism which would give us reprieve from the pain and anguish which we both needed in order to function. Being on the cruise distracted us somewhat. Often however the reality would insidiously make its way in and remove us from the bliss of this state of denial. That is how it was for me anyway.

There were moments on the cruise where the pain was unbearable for me. I would do my best to protect Phil from seeing these moments of despair. How could I let him see this? The entire scenario was too surreal for me; there was a disbelief that it was even happening, surely not to us, not in my life; this did not happen to me but to others. These times of despair would arise when I would come out of my state of denial and be absolutely in the moment, in the harsh reality of what was happening in our lives.

The shower in our cabin was very confined and this became my place where I could go and weep, no, not weep, but shed hard long tears in a silence that was necessary. The water from the shower would disguise my tears as the two joined and streamed down my body. Protecting Phil from seeing this was necessary. If he was still in a place of denial or disbelief or absolute blind faith in God then who was I to take him away from any sanctuary that he had?

One night whilst at sea we went to a fabulous show, and Phil was laughing loudly in his infectious laugh that he had. Phil had a huge roaring laugh that everyone loved, and this alone would invite others to join in also—often not laughing at the joke but at Phil as he laughed and also clapped his hands at the same time.

As I stood back slightly from Phil and watched him I thought, Thank You God that Phil can laugh and is feeling such joy at this present moment. A part of me so wished that I too could let go and feel this happiness, but I could not and would not allow myself to, that night. The thoughts that were going through my mind were that Phil enjoy every minute of this life on earth. I felt terrible knowing that these were memories and moments for recollection later—memories that I would not be sharing with Phil in the future but quietly reflecting to myself, sharing with others, or as I am doing now, documenting them so that they can form part of this story. I do not have the right words to convey what I felt at that moment as I watched him enjoying this show apart from describing it as a deep sadness that I had not experienced before, not for myself, but for Phil.

Another vivid memory for me was as we sat in the centre of the ship where the stairwell spiralled down. Phil and I sat in a booth holding hands and listening to the live band and watched others dance to the music. I escaped into my own little fantasy of the beautiful women who would have been on the final voyage of the Titanic as they came down the stairwell in their elegant gowns. Occasionally I would sneak a look at Phil to see how he was as we sat in silence much of that evening, both of us I am sure wanting to protect the other from talking about the third party that hovered in the booth with us.

How I wished so much that it was only the two of us in this booth and not the presence of those three words, *small cell carcinoma*, that appeared on that piece of paper which was in our cabin—this piece of paper that I was able to visualize in an instant, word for word and which was embedded my mind.

One night we attended a live show that had music playing from one of my favourite old bands ABBA and Phil got up to get closer to the stage as the music and dancers had begun their energetic show. Again this terrible sadness engulfed me. As I watched Phil I could not help but think to myself, enjoy this time Phil as I was not sure how many more we would share like this. It was as if he did not have a care in the world as he stood there clapping to the music, watching the live show and moving his body freely.

If only I had that much control over my body. The fear had once again taken over. All I could do was sit in the booth, my body trembling, as I attempted to remove the thoughts from my mind that this would be the last time that Phil and I would experience a cruise together, that this would be one of the last times I would see Phil so happy. At that moment, deep in my heart, I knew this to be a fact. Similar to that day prior to his diagnosis when I was walking in the sun and seeing his funeral, I knew that my precious husband would die.

Phil was laughing and clapping, and I could not help but wonder if he was not facing the reality of what we had been told that week. Had he now fallen that much into denial, or was his faith so strong that he had simply handed his fate over to God? As I watched a part of me envied his state and longed that I too could escape into it. However, I felt immense gratitude also for what I was observing. Phil was enjoying himself and was not someone whom had already died inside. Phil still had this positive outlook and would not allow the fear to take him over as obviously as it had done for me at that time.

For the first time since the diagnosis real anger engrossed me as I watched Phil in his own beautiful world that he had created for himself. I was not angry at God or at Phil but at everyone in the room and on the dance floor who were drinking, laughing and having fun. How dare they, I thought; don't you know what is happening in this very room, don't you know the pain I am feeling? The fact that everyone was laughing and was oblivious to my pain created anger in me that I did not quite know what to do with. Why was it that we were handed this straw, the shortest of them all, whilst others were all able to enjoy this cruise, just as we were supposed to. I felt so robbed and angry at everyone as their lives had not altered, but Phil's and mine had now changed forever.

We took many photos on this trip, and I have since created an album specifically of this holiday, a process which was part of my healing. One of the most beautiful photos was of a statue of Our Lady that we had discovered outside a Catholic Church in the Bahamas. This church was surrounded by the most beautiful array of colors from many varieties of flowers that were on the church grounds. Phil and I knelt together before this statue, and in silence we prayed our own requests, both praying I am sure, no—begging for the same thing. We placed our trust totally in God and Our Lady. Being away from New Zealand and finding this most beautiful statue hidden away in the Caribbean was yet another sign to us that we were being held and that our prayers were being heard.

Our original plan was to leave mainland USA and have a few days in Hawaii on the way home. However, we decided that it would be best to go home sooner so that Phil could then go ahead with the scheduled CT scan and find where else in his body this cancer was. Quietly I was relieved to be going home as I felt that time was not on our side. Somehow I felt more in control of the situation. I have since learned that with cancer there is often no such thing has having control.

Travelling back to Los Angeles from Fort Lauderdale was a very long day, and we arrived in our hotel room totally exhausted. We were to leave Los Angeles the following evening which gave us a day together, so we decided to go shopping, something that Phil and I both loved and did well together.

We would go our separate ways and meet up every couple of hours for a food break and to compare shopping bags. Phil loved his clothes and was not shy in spending up on himself, something I was thrilled about. He had an incredible patience with me and on many occasions would end up looking like an overloaded donkey like they do back in Croatia. He was carrying all of my shopping bags that I would load him up with. On one occasion, as we were leaving Hawaii, poor Phil had to wear three layers of clothing in the Pacific heat including on board the flight home since there was no way that we could get all of our shopping into our suitcases.

This final day of our holiday was a good one for me as I fell into a day of denial. In fact, I feel that we both did. I took myself into the shopping and pretended that all was fine. There was an excitement about going home to Phil's recovery and to our summer together. It was blissful leaving the darkness behind for a few hours and shopping for summer clothes.

My reality momentarily returned as Phil told me that he did not know what to shop for, "Would I need business shirts or just some casual clothes? I don't know if I will be working for much longer." I immediately dismissed that thought as I did when we were on the ship. I asked him one day what I could get him for his birthday and his words to me were "Tarn, the only birthday present I want is to see another birthday."

During Phil's illness there were some words spoken by him that I just cannot forget, and this sentence was one of them. It was like a stabbing into my chest as Phil voiced his deepest fear, especially now when I reflect on these words and wonder if, on some deep level, Phil had a chilling knowledge of what the final outcome would be.

Phil was scheduled to have a CT scan as soon as possible after our arrival home. We also received news that his blood tests once again appeared normal and did not show the primary cancer. We were both very naïve and felt that this was a good thing.

On the day of the CT scan the doctor informed us that on the scan there was no sign of any other cancer in Phil's body; hence they did not know where the primary cancer was. Quietly we were happy, and we chose not to take notice of the look of concern on this doctor's face as he wished Phil well on his journey. We drove away feeling ecstatic. Yes, there was no primary tumor which means that there was only this lump under his armpit and a couple in his chest. Once these disappear then he will be fine. We were totally in that blissful state of denial. This was what we chose to believe. As yet we did not have a complete understanding about this type of cancer and the seriousness of his diagnosis. After all, no one had yet mentioned the word *death* or *number of months*, nor did we ask.

Whatever this state was, it was working for us at this time, and we shared our happiness. Phil phoned his sister in the car and my parents also to inform them of the good news. Oh how little we really knew at that time of what small cell carcinoma of unknown primary really meant.

That day I returned home and went into our bedroom and prayed thanking God for taking care of us and how I would be forever grateful for a positive outcome and that a life of dedication to doing good was what I would do. My bargaining with God had begun. This was all we could cope with. The thought or remote possibility that Phil would die and that our life as we knew it would come to an end was just not conceivable for us. I could not imagine any reason for Phil to be taken so soon from this life when he had influenced the lives of so many already, so why even entertain the thought.

The day before the CT Scan Phil informed his boss and good friend, Dave, of his diagnosis and would most probably need to resign. This was not easy for Phil. As I watched him desperately trying to hold himself together, he shared his story with Dave. Part of me wanted him to let out the pain and not hold back but, knowing Phil, whilst he was in work mode, this would not have been the professional thing to do.

Well after the scan and our wonderful news Phil made the decision not to resign from work. He would continue his battle with the cancer and continue with life as normal, "It won't be an issue" were his words!

FOUR

Blind Faith

Friday December 3 we received a letter in the post from Phil's oncologist summarizing the results of the scan and the options now available for Phil, which were chemotherapy followed by a course of radiotherapy. Due to not knowing the location of the primary cancer meant first treating Phil for lung cancer and if that was not successful then trying another type of chemotherapy to see if this had more of an effect on the tumors. In this letter the oncologist mentioned the response rate of treatment for this type of cancer, which by the way was not favorable.

Once again my fear was triggered. If only people would leave us alone and not keep giving us statistics and information, we would remain in our own world of trust and faith and in what we choose to believe. Phil saw my distress whilst home for lunch that day, and he too read the letter and did a very good job of hiding his concern.

As Phil was eating his lunch at the table, I could not sit, and I could not eat. I loaded the wash into the machine, and I cried. I was unable to disguise this crippling fear even for a moment. He hated to see me distressed or show any sign of fear as he needed me to be positive so that it enabled him to also remain positive. I wondered if Phil interpreted the meaning of this letter as I did or was he once again being strong for me and holding onto his blind faith.

Phil headed back out to work that afternoon and phoned our home to leave a message for me. He was feeling strong, rather jovial in fact, and was receiving comfort in some way which he wanted to share with me. This was his phone message at 1.19 P.M. on that first Friday of December:

Tanya, it's Phil! Tanya, just remember we are on a journey honey. All this stuff that is coming in is about a journey from God. Take on board the closeness of prayer that we have had, how the priest has been with us, how the parish has been with us, how we are being able to help other people. What is happening with things like David Chaloner [our friend and my therapist] and everything I am doing to beat this—this is all to make us better people, and I guess for me to make me a more confident person in the world to see who I am. I am dealing with stress a lot better. I am not worrying about nothing. It isn't worth it, and at the end of the day I am in a very free position, because I can just say "Stuff it; I don't want to put up with this." So don't let the written word from a doctor upset you honey. The only written word that we have to check is from the Bible. He is the great and divine healer, end of story, and I believe totally in Him.

Whenever I would listen to this message from Phil, before and after his death, I felt one could not speak such truer words which he held onto the entire time. I believe totally in Him. These words to this day continue to strengthen me during my times of despair.

Around this time we had close friends over for a barbeque, and Phil had decided to make the announcement to everyone of what was happening in his life. I observed them all as he shared his news and was so saddened by the look of shock on their faces. Many of these people had worked with Phil for years and to hear such news would have devastated them. "Not Phil, not our mentor. He will be fine, nothing could possibly happen to Phil," I heard.

Phil and I received a gift that afternoon which was a set of his and her aluminum garden ornaments that looked like a sunflower however with a ceramic centre. Phil's was blue and mine was red. Later that month we found that the blue ceramic centre from Phil's sunflower ornament had mysteriously broken off. This was now the third thing that had broken of

Phil's in as many weeks and it scared me as I tried to dismiss any form of superstition from penetrating my thinking.

Such occurrences would normally not alarm me, but I was hypersensitive to everything that was happening around me at this time and would keep looking for a sign—any sign that all would be well for us. One of the most difficult things for me at this time was the feeling of absolute powerlessness and lack of control, the unknown. Then again I would wonder if this was the time when I would once again have to surrender all control over to God and let His will be done.

It was that same afternoon we received a phone call from Phil's oncologist who informed us of Phil's options: he could commence chemotherapy immediately followed by radiotherapy or he could go to Melbourne to have another scan called a PET scan. This had the ability to detect tumors on the lung which may not be visible with the CT scan which did not show anything at this point. As chemotherapy was just not an option for Phil he decided that we go to Melbourne the following week to discover where, if anywhere, this other tumor was hiding in his body.

On December 5, a Sunday afternoon, Phil and I went to visit friends, Sue and Michelle. Michelle had a lot of knowledge about cancer as she was in the helping profession and was recommending to Phil that he do everything possible to fight this cancer. "Everything, throw everything at it," she said. She offered to look up on the internet what small cell carcinoma really was and to provide us with some knowledge on this type of cancer. Phil agreed as this was something that we chose not to do ourselves, somehow knowing not to.

The following afternoon as I was sitting at my office desk I received a phone call from Michelle to let me know she and Sue would be coming over that night to inform us of what she now understood about this type of cancer. Michelle warned me that the news was not good, and Phil needed to consider all options for his path. I knew my time of grace was about to end. My times of denial would become less and less and that soon fear would be always present in my world.

The next twenty-four hours were a little short of hell on earth for both of us. Michelle and Sue arrived and after our pleasantries we all sat around the dining room table as if we were having a board meeting. I knew what was coming as Michelle brought out her internet printouts and placed them on the table. Oh how I wanted her to read to us that this cancer was curable, one hundred percent success rate, please. Let me just have this little fantasy for a few seconds before you give us this heavy blow which I knew was coming.

Michelle began to read the papers to us. Every time she gave us more facts and statistics on small cell carcinoma of unknown primary she would stop and feel the need to somehow make these words easier for us. She would look up at us and qualify what was written by saying "These statistics were more for men in an older age group, not a young fit healthy man like you Phil. You have the strength to fight this Phil however you must throw everything you can at this cancer." What Michelle meant was that Phil needed to consider traditional treatment.

Both Phil and I were silent as we listened to Michelle quietly and softly continue to read her findings to us. For me it felt as though I was on another plain, having removed myself from my physical body and looking down upon this frightened young woman as if she was sitting in a courtroom having a life sentence of horror being read to her.

Phil was very brave and stoic during this time however it was when Sue handed over a gift for Phil—one of the T-shirts that belonged to her late husband and Phil's friend—that he was overwhelmed and his tears came, as did Sue and Michelle's. He said that he would wear it to give him good luck when he goes to Melbourne for his PET scan, which he did.

Phil had embraced Sue's children over the past few years and would frequently take them to rugby league games to watch their local heroes the Warriors. Phil's tears became stronger as he told Sue that he could not bear the thought of her son losing another dad. His emotion was present, and he allowed it to be at this time.

As painful as this scene was for me, I did not cry. Somehow, I would find strength when I saw Phil's pain, and knowing his nature I felt that I needed to hold in my feelings to allow him to express and feel his. I did not want him to always feel this need to be so brave and courageous for everyone all of the time. He was there for me when I fell apart, and, when he needed to do the same, whilst I could not explain to you where my strength would come from, I was able to be there for him.

We were both in shock and holding our emotions in as we walked our guests out rather formally as if the business meeting had just come to an end. Without speaking a word about what had just happened, Phil and I came inside, cleaned up in the kitchen and went to bed. We lay there in the dark in our usual position of my head being nestled into his left armpit, and we both began to voice our deepest fears.

Phil just did not want to have any traditional treatment and commented on how he had visions of himself like his late uncle, on a white slab, thin and pale, and in the end he still may not survive this ordeal. Phil often commented that he did not want to glow in his casket as a result of traditional treatment.

All of a sudden the worst heaviness came upon my chest. My life seemed black and no longer worth living. My horror was beating at my head, and I then began to fall apart in our bed with Phil's arms around me. Phil held me as I cried out loud from the depths of my being. My emotion was so strong it hurt to release it. Phil just held me and gave me permission to release this feeling that I had never experienced before. I could only describe it as a terror of what I felt was awaiting us, awaiting me, for the rest of my life.

Phil just kept saying to me "let it out." He unselfishly let me fall apart to a degree that I don't believe I did again in front of him. This I knew had to be the final time to do this as from this day on I had to be strong for this man.

This was truly a dark night for us both, and we barely slept. However once again we arose early, and Phil headed off to the gym as normal presenting to everyone that all was well in his world. I was weak and terrified and needed to gather strength, and all I knew to do was to go to morning mass and once again connect with my God.

Normally I would sit in our normal seat at the front of the church, however on this morning I could not as I needed to be alone with our Lord with no one around me, begging Him in silence to release us from this horror. I sat toward the back of the church where on the right hand side in a small alcove was a beautiful statue of Jesus with His arms reaching out. I sat as close as possible to this statue somehow feeling that He was holding me, or that His peace was beaming from His outstretched arms onto me and covering me, protecting me.

Nothing could alleviate my pain that morning or stop my tears as I explained to the local nun that Phil's cancer was aggressive. Her response to me was, "May His will be done and may He give you the strength to accept it." Whilst deep in my heart I knew these words to be true I did not want to believe or accept them. The reality was that I had no other options at this point but to accept it, or to once again fall into my abyss of hope and faith, or was it denial? It was the latter that I chose that day.

Phil phoned me during the day with the decision that he was not going to listen to anyone else or what the internet said—and totally trust God in this entire process. I was relieved to hear his strength. At that point I was not sure what state Phil was in, whether he was experiencing shock or denial or if it was exactly what he had voiced to me—purely and simply total surrender to God's will and that blind faith we always went back to. Yes, I agreed with him. Let's not listen to anything anyone else has to say but to totally rest our lives in God's hands, and this was what we did.

December 10 we flew to Melbourne for the day for this PET scan and on this day Phil proudly wore the T-shirt that once belonged to his late friend for good luck.

Sitting still was not my greatest attribute, and this was all I was able to do during this long day during the flights and whilst waiting for Phil during his scan. I drowned myself in prayer, and, in the midst of all that tension during this sixteen hours, I felt at peace. It felt very strange sitting in this cancer centre, knowing that all of us in the waiting room were either suffering from cancer or had a loved one who was. We shared a common bond, one which we all felt in spite of no words needing to be exchanged. It was a bond that I did not want to be a part of, and I wondered if on some level I had not yet truly accepted that I was a part of it holding onto the belief that our story would be different than theirs.

There was closeness between Phil and I that nothing could sever. On that day we were on a mission together with God walking right by our side. He felt positive and felt great when undressing for his scan. He was informed by the nurse that he could leave his T-shirt on. Phil was overwhelmed by this as it was his good luck charm. Whilst lying on the table about to be scanned, on the radio came his current favourite song by U2,

"It's a Beautiful Day," one which he knew his friend loved also. Phil felt as though he was being taken care of by his angel in heaven at that time, and I had no doubt that he was.

December 14 was our eighth wedding anniversary which as always we celebrated out to dinner, however it was the following day that was of significance to us. It was the night when we met with the oncologist to discuss the results of the PET scan. Just before our appointment we had dinner at my cousin's home, Ivan and Vesna, together with my parents which was perfect. It provided us with a distraction and even some laughter. What I do remember about this night is the seafood risotto that Vesna made and how Phil enjoyed it so much. He ate a lot of food that night and this cancer thing was not going to stop him and his love of food.

Once seated together in the waiting area, the tension was present for us both as we held hands and silently prayed. For Phil these results would be the deciding factor on his decision regarding his treatment. His mind was already made up. When the oncologist informed Phil that there was no sign of a primary cancer Phil's words to him were, "I could hug you." I too was overjoyed at this result. I still did not truly understand what small cell carcinoma of unknown primary really meant, or perhaps I simply did not want to know. We knew that Phil was not completely healthy, but despite our lack of understanding the doctor did not clarify this matter for us, and we left his office in gleeful ignorance.

The doctors were all aware of how Phil felt about the traditional treatment option and knew not to push him into anything. That night we had a plan. It was to allow the oncologist to give us the treatment options, and I would take notes as Phil asked questions, and no decision would be made that night in the meeting. Once Phil knew that the primary was nowhere to be found I knew that he had made his mind up in that instant. No words needed to be exchanged between us; I knew what his feelings were on the matter.

The following day we went to morning Mass and the Psalm read on this day was Psalm 30. I wept when I heard the words. Phil also heard these words and we both felt it was God telling us that everything would be alright. "Weeping may go on all night, but in the morning there is joy." We both gained a lot of strength from the words to this Psalm during the following months, and it soon became our favourite. It was not until Phil had passed did I truly understand the depth of the meaning to this Psalm and how it was to play such a significant part in my healing and surrender. This Psalm was read at Phil's funeral.

From that evening on we decided to live as though life was normal for us and not of a couple living with the dread and fear of cancer. Within weeks however Phil developed a rather severe bruising down his entire left side which reminded us that there was no such thing as normal when you were living with cancer. We were later to learn that this was the cancer on the move, and it was well ahead of us.

A short while before Christmas Phil decided to go on a very rigid diet mainly of raw foods which proved to be very stressful for him especially for someone who loved his food. Being such a large man he needed a lot of food to keep his strength up, so he became weaker and started to lose weight and looked somewhat gaunt in the face. He had such beautiful cheek bones, and they began to show even more. Life for me became one of sourcing foods, juicing, preparing meals and obsessively doing what I could to assist in his healing—all of which became exhausting, but it was a tiredness that did not register for me. I had learned to exist on pure adrenalin.

In spite of the commercialism of Christmas it has always been a special time for Phil and I. There was always a far greater meaning for us. Once December arrived the excitement and carol music would begin and so would my preparation for this celebration. This was a very busy time of year for Phil. Being in the grocery industry he was often rushed off his feet as everyone began their preparations for the Christmas feasts. Some of my sadness around this time of year was that he was not able to enjoy the lead up to Christmas day. It was not until Christmas Eve that he would sit back and relax with a beer into holiday mode.

How different would this Christmas have been for us had we known it would be the final one we would share? What would it have been like? Thankfully, without this knowledge we continued to hold onto the hope and blind faith that we both had in God's will for us.

Christmas Eve would be my most favourite day, particularly midnight Mass. This year was especially beautiful. Not only were my parents there, but also Zel and his wife, Delwyn, with their children and my girlfriend Jo. Phil and I always had a ritual of coming home from Mass, opening one present each and having a glass of port. Nothing was different this year. "Blow the diet," Phil said as he had his port!

I don't remember what gifts we exchanged that evening; however I remember the surprise he had for me the following morning. After we had opened our presents on Christmas morning in our usual manner, one each at a time, Phil then went away and came back with a beautifully wrapped box, and inside it was a gorgeous amethyst necklace on a gold chain. The Christmas card that came with the amethyst had an angel on it. He addressed the card to *his healing angel,* and his words were that whenever he looked into this stone when I wore it, he would be healing himself of his cancer.

Phil really spoiled me with gifts that Christmas. I felt that he wanted to do something special, however his generosity did scare me somewhat. I wondered if he knew on a deep level that this would be the last we would share together. Did he want to leave me with some special memories of this as our final Christmas?

Writing in a journal has been a practice for me since I was in my teens, and to this day continues to be a method of healing. However during Phil's illness I found it very difficult to write after learning of his lump on October 24 2004. It was not until two months later on Christmas Eve that I was able to put pen to paper once again. "It is now Christmas Eve 2004 and I feel it is time for me to commence this story, however I keep procrastinating because I don't want to feel the pain that writing brings."

On January 6 I was not coping and once again the pain was with me as I wrote, "I feel so terrible, I'm up and down and I just cannot function. Part of the reason is because I am so tired and life is just so busy for me. I cannot think straight."

It was some time in December that Phil also began to document in his journal what he entitled, *My Journey,* and so his profound words began:

What has my tumor got to teach me? I am going to get this handled. I pray with all my heart to allow me to finally face whatever is stored inside the tumor. I am finally ready to face it and let it go.

We have bodies, minds and emotions but mostly what we are is soul—something that cannot be touched, tested or surgically removed. Everyone must follow their own unique healing path. Spiritual transformation is an inner journey, the soul's personal path of learning and letting go, something that must be experienced on your own. Philip, this Cancer is a gift, not only for me but to others who could benefit from what you discover. Help me to find a prayer that allows me to heal physically, emotionally and spiritually. What if, instead of reframing my emotions I simply welcomed them and allowed them to be fully felt. I wonder if I might find the peace in the core of the feeling. In the face of emotion, don't move; welcome it. Why would I seek love from others when I'd realized *I am love?*

I have been compelled with a need to help and serve people even though it has cost me my health. It was when I was giving to others and helping them in some way that I felt my best. You have suppressed exhaustion buried in your cells. You are just going to have to wait this one out and rest and heal. How do you plan to be around to help others if you are not willing to take care of yourself? If you don't stop, your body will stop you. I need to face one of the biggest issues of my life to examine my very identity and to find out what has been driving me.

In the face of emotion, don't move, welcome it.
The way of love is not a subtle argument. The door there is devastation.
Birds make great sky, circles of their freedom.
How do they learn it?
They fall, and in falling, they are given wings.

What followed was a letter that Phil wrote to his current self from his future self which he noted was a part of his inner healing.

Dear Self. At this time, when the knowledge that you have cancer is very raw and frightening to you, I want the present you to understand

that such things as illness like this are very often for the good of you giving into the future. I am letting you know that I will be there for you with
every new step you take in renewing yourself, your beliefs and your
patterns for handling and living life. During this time and for all time
trust God, give yourself over to Him and pray every day for His guidance and wisdom to enter and direct your life. Be one with God. With
every decision you make tune into his magnificence and ask for divine
direction.

FIVE

Signs

The summer which we both loved had finally arrived, and the heat of January meant that we wore lighter clothing and spent much time outdoors in our garden. So often Phil would be out there with his shirt off appearing to not have a care at all about the changes that were happening to his body, or was it that he was a master at disguising his feelings to his very sensitive angel?

I continued to watch his body like a hawk hovering over its prey, seeing if there was any sign of a change. I memorized every bump and mark and continued to quietly scan his body in the hope that he would not notice my concerns. My feelings would sway from absolute peace and trust that he would survive this cancer in a flash to losing that peace, falling into that crippling fear and then escaping back into the denial which was often all that my conscious mind could handle. Anything could trigger this change in my feelings, however now it was noticing his body changing before my very eyes that would be the catalyst for this downfall in my emotional state. "I let go and let God," I wrote in mid January. However how quickly my fear would return as I wrote but two days later, "I have to constantly fight the fear" and then two days later again on the Tuesday night January 25, "the fear is back. I am seeing that Phil's lymph nodes are getting bigger rather than smaller. Even though I have so many positive things to hold on to, still I am frightened. Dear Lord, hear my pleas."

Phil commenced his new journal on January 11, one that I bought him for Christmas a few days earlier. It had a silver cover with a Maori design on the front, and this was the beginning of Phil's journal that he told me would make up a considerable amount of the book that he was planning to write about his journey when he recovered.

Having three cats in the house was a lot of fun, however it was also a constant gripe as they also caused considerable mess and havoc! Rudi and Fergus were incredibly competitive and continued to fight each other for our attention. Phil had quite a soft spot for the naughty Fergus who had only twelve months earlier joined our home and very quickly had become my baby.

The first entry in Phil's new journal I found rather humorous as he vented his frustration at the cats.

I sat down at 10 P.M. but had to clean up and deodorize the corner as Fergus has pissed on my healing corner! I feel agitated and angry about this. The thing that tops this off is the fact that he is such a beautiful, loving cat and is so much Tanya's baby replacement. To banish him outside would be impossible. We would end up in divorce, and I could not bring myself to do it anyway.

I will never forget Saturday January 30 as it was a day when the tensions between us arose, and we took it out on each other. Fighting for us was very rare. In fact I could probably count on one hand during our ten years together the number of times we had raised our voices to one another. It was so infrequent that we could never fight with a straight face, and often one of us would just walk away. When it was me all I wanted to do was laugh at how ridiculous the fight was in the first place.

For me the feeling surrounding our disagreement was one of desperation. Underneath the pain of us not being on good terms that day was also the fear deep in my being that things were deteriorating for Phil. Why were these lumps getting bigger, why were there more lumps, what was in these lumps, and why would Phil discount them and not want to engage in the reality of what I was seeing?

The tension that arose between us that day had resulted from us both seeing the obvious physical changes happening to his body whilst both wanting to protect the other from our fears by not voicing them but allowing the tension to build. This boil however needed to explode, and as a result it enabled us to once again come together on this journey and to remain united during the highs and lows. January 30 was the last time we raised our voices at one another, and in my desperation I surrendered again to God that afternoon: "I went to Mass today and prayed for awhile which then resulted in the rest of my day being filled with a peace in my heart, a God given peace."

As a result of Phil's decision to not take treatment in the form of chemotherapy or radiotherapy people would often speak to me of this and give me their opinions. They were actually projecting their own fears onto me, and it was not something I would cope with well nor share with Phil. What it did do however was to generate a heightened level of fear within me, especially since I had visible evidence of what was happening to Phil's body as I continued my scanning. I grew to know every new mark, every new lump and its size, and to me it became obvious that the cancer was moving very fast.

Holding in my concerns when I saw changes, was very difficult. One night when Phil was sitting at the dining room table, I noticed a large lump just above his left collar bone. It was an obvious change and threw me into an immediate panic—one I was not able to keep to myself. Phil became rather annoyed at my reaction. However I just could not but help voice my concerns which so often Phil did not like. He needed to do things his way and what felt right for him, without the input of others and at times me also.

Phil writes in his journal a few days after our fight,

Tanya has lightened a hell of a lot since Saturday's blow up. I know she has been churning over because of approaches from other people about my no go chemotherapy. She is getting chemo conversation from all sides. Tanya has taken on so much since my diagnosis that I am worried about burnout. I would like to see her strengthen up all four sides of her so that no doubt can impregnate and create the disharmony as it does. I have seen the intenseness in my girl for three to four weeks now. This does worry me, because I fear for such things as a nervous breakdown. I really have to encourage self care for her as I need her well, alive and loving.

Phil had such a concern for me during this time when I had none at all for myself as all of my energy was invested in what was happening to his body, both internally and externally. It was not until just before his death did my exhaustion begin to surface for me and after his death the emotional burnout also finally appeared.

Phil and I lived in Jervois Road for nine years and it was a home that we bought together and grew to love immensely especially the suburb as it was so close to the Harbor. We loved the beautiful gardens we had created and many joyous memories that were also created there. At times we had decided to sell and made some serious noises about doing so however were never able to go through with it because of our love of the home.

On February 4 however we were given an offer for our home and accepted it almost immediately as we needed to sell in order to provide funds if and when Phil was to stop working. So this offer was given to us at the perfect time by the perfect buyer. We were thrilled at who was purchasing our home and unbeknown to us at the time she became such an angel in our journey and in mine to follow for many months.

In spite of what we were faced with, Phil and I had a deep belief that we were being taken care of and finally letting go of our home was meant to be part of the plan of this journey of ours. We were always astounded at the unbelievable synchronicity that took place for the weeks leading up to the sale of our home, and it confirmed to us again that we were to finally let it go and move forward with our lives in whatever direction it would take.

In early February we went to Australia for a few days and by this time Phil's left arm had started to swell. In fact I noticed this slight change during one of my secretive scans of his body a couple of weeks earlier. Phil did not tell me about it and tried to hide it from me, however this hawk spotted it the moment he had taken his shirt off in front of me one day. From my basic knowledge I knew that it was lymphoedema, and I just could not keep my mouth shut. I immediately mentioned it to him, and deeply I knew this was not a good sign. I could also see that more lumps were appearing in places where they were not before, hence my fear was now escalating to an all time high.

The night before we left on our trip to Australia Catherine was once again there with us and ready to take care of the three cats. When Phil showered later in the evening I was in my office with her and my tears began to pour out of me as I finally faced my fear of losing Phil. For the first time I voiced to Catherine what was now a reality for me. I spoke to her of my fear as I witnessed the changes in Phil's body, and her words to me were, "perhaps on some level Tanya you know that Phil is not going to make it."

Hearing Catherine voice these words, which were in fact my truth, was for me surrender to my deepest belief that one day, sooner rather than later, Phil would be leaving me. I was finally admitting and facing what I intuitively knew was going to happen, that Phil was dying. Paralysis enveloped me as I let my tears explode out of my being whilst she was in my office. I had to do this as quietly and as quickly as I could so that Phil would not hear me. For that brief moment I left my sanctuary of denial and felt my greatest pain of losing Phil to this insidious disease that was now beginning to ravage his beautiful body.

This emotional pain accompanied by a bout of food poisoning made for an awful night and an even worse trip to Sydney the following day. Everything was all the more intolerable for me. My defenses were down, and by the time we arrived at our destination I was so full of fear that I could barely function. Phil believed it was only the food poisoning that had taken me down so rapidly. I had not yet been able to shake my darkness; it was still with me no matter how much I wanted my trusted friend *denial* to return. I wrote, "I feel desperate as my fear has escalated and my state of mind is just unbearable. All I can do is talk to God as nothing else would move this mountain."

During the next three days I pleaded continuously to God to carry me though this horror. Without Him I could not function. My only vision was a never-ending abyss of darkness.

Once again through my continued prayer, peace arrived—or had I once again taken myself into my sanctuary of denial? Whatever my state was, all that mattered was the return of my absolute faith and belief that Phil would survive as I wrote,

> It is 5 A.M. in Sydney at the Stamford Plaza, and we have just had an awesome weekend. The past two days have been completely away from fear of which I will now hold on to as much as I can. The alternative is purgatory for me.

This was how I truly felt at that time. There was this unbelievable strength and belief inside me that Phil would survive, in spite of the obvious physical changes. What I was actually holding on to was blind faith that God would come through with a miracle as there was absolutely no logical reason why Phil would not make it. He had far too much to offer in this life. My defense mechanism of denial was kicking in strong and hard.

By the time we returned from Australia Phil's arm had changed size and shape considerably as did his left side and it was at this time he decided to see his doctor whom he trusted so much to see what could be done to alleviate the swelling. Phil knew that Rhona would not push the traditional treatment avenue. When she mentioned it Phil would not even entertain the thought even though it was becoming so obvious now that all was not well. This was his body and his call, and he knew that she respected his feelings.

Seeing his concern and fear now more clearly was always harder for me than to feel my own. Somehow I could cope with my pain far better than seeing Phil's as I did that day in Rhona's office.

At this point not only did Phil have more lumps in his lymph nodes with the new one around his collar bone getting larger by the day, but his left arm at this stage was now very swollen, and each of his fingers were beginning to slightly swell. His left side was starting to look somewhat larger and the nodes in his left groin had already swollen at this point.

I was unaware of the pain that he was experiencing until I read his journal after his passing. He wrote on February 11, "I am very sore in the groin and my left shoulder. Carry the cross with Grace and Strength." February 15 Phil wrote "Goodbye my beautiful friend Kevin who died three years ago today. I loved you." Phil would be seeing his beautiful friend within eight weeks of this entry.

As part of my need to process my feelings I commenced something called a gratitude journal and every night I would try to find something to be grateful for in my day in order to keep up a positive attitude. Phil also commenced such a journal as recommended by a friend. Reading it since his death has been a continued source of strength for me to see how even in the adversity he was facing he was always able to find something to be grateful for in his day.

On February 14 I wrote "I am grateful today that my husband is alive and feels well. I am also grateful for sharing another Valentine's Day with Philip." The following day I wrote that "I feel grateful that I have had a day free of fear." It was the fear that would constantly cripple me, so a day without it was a day in heaven, however it was something I battled each moment of everyday.

February 16 I write, "Phil has told me that his glands in his right groin were now also swollen. I felt some fear but have not really thought about it much today." This was my denial. I so desperately wanted to hold the hope I had gained whilst we were away—the belief that no matter what was happening before my eyes, Phil would survive, and we would be granted a miracle.

Those who knew Phil would have remembered him for his infectious laugh and very dry sense of humour. He had an unbelievable gift of putting his feelings down on paper in the form of poetry, and his humour would often come out this way, as it often did in his journaling even during this tumultuous time. My favourite entry was February 19. The first time I read this it really did make me laugh.

I am very tired. Didn't sleep very well at all, and I think that was due to the disappointment of the cricket! I cannot believe that with eleven balls and eleven runs that we lost!

Phil and I both prayed every night before our meal, and Phil's words always were, "Thank You Lord for healing me of this cancer." It was during these days when the signs were appearing rather rapidly that he would add to this prayer, "if it be Your will."

When the fear would come, instead of allowing it to be visible whilst in Phil's company, I learned other ways of coping with it. Often it was by voicing it to a select few in my support network who were able to carry me when I was feeling low. One of those was to my eldest brother Zel.

Zel had such an inner strength to draw on in times of crisis and was such a rock for me as I was growing up—someone whom I would turn to for protection and comfort. Here I was again often like a little girl so full of fear and needing comfort from my big brother. A beautiful email from Zel came to me on March 4 when I was feeling particularly low.

> You know what to do when the fear wave hits. Think of Christ's fear in the Garden on Holy Thursday. All I can do is love you and Phil with all my heart and ask God for his infinite assistance. Remember, all saints suffer on earth. You guys are saints amidst the chosen few.

This email was one that made me weep and weep and still brings much emotion to me when I read these words eighteen months after I first read them. I can only imagine his pain and feelings of powerlessness whilst writing these words.

Six

Bargaining

During March Phil and I had another brief overseas trip planned however, he decided that it was not the right time and that when he was well enough we would travel together again soon. He was insistent that I still go, mainly to rejuvenate my own strength and spirit.

Phil did not tell me at this stage he was beginning to feel physical pain, and neither of us at this point thought that he would deteriorate as quickly as he did over the next five weeks. Had I known I would not have left for those seven days, those seven precious days.

What going away did was give me time to build up my energy for what lay ahead of me physically and emotionally for the month after my return. It gave me even a greater sense of hope than I had had for a long time. Upon my return I was strong and had absolute faith in God and still an absolute belief that Phil would live, that there would be a miracle that Phil would get to write about in his journey as he so wanted to.

This time was beneficial for Phil as it gave him time to sit and truly be with himself and his God, to reflect with no other interruptions, simply be at peace in the silence that was surrounding him.

One of his gym buddies, Rod, often said to me how brave Phil was and how he often said to Rod, "Don't worry about me mate. This is between me and the big fella upstairs."

March 8 I flew out and during my flight I began to write in my journal more extensively.

Yesterday when I left Phil looked sad at the airport, and it felt tough to say goodbye. It is nice to leave home for a break as I am at a breaking point myself, totally exhausted. However I am also aware of what I am coming back to and the reality of what I have just left behind. I wish that Phil's swelling was less. I am fearful that he is getting worse. however, it is hope that I hold—the hope that everyone else has also. This is what I must hold onto. I am excited about our new tranquil life together when I return.

Once in my hotel room I wrote, "I miss Phil so much. Oh God, help me in my pain. I am now wondering if this is how it will be for me in the future."

This was the final entry I made in my journal until after Phil's funeral. Once I returned home from this trip on March 15, my world, which was my life with Phil, was slipping through my tightly clenched fingers.

Whilst I was away things changed for Phil dramatically, and it was not until I read his journal that I discovered how things really were for him during this time and how tightly he clung to God for strength. How I wished that he had shared it with me, but Phil, not being one to worry me, would keep things to himself.

We spoke on the phone daily, and he shared nothing about his decline during these calls. Once again we were both protecting the other from our fears. Was this a good thing I ask myself, or should I have been more insistent on sharing my fears? Did he instinctively know not to share with me what was happening to him?

Why was it that his rapid decline happened literally on the night I left the country? Had it started before I was due to leave, I never would have left him. Would he have even told me I wonder? It was only some time after Phil's passing did I truly see the big picture. This time was very much Phil's time to truly connect with his God and to come to a point of acceptance on some level of his fate.

What I can share of that week during my absence was the journey as it was for Phil, in his words. Phil's journal entry on the night I left, March 9 read,

My dear God, please help me to recover my health back to one hundred percent. I don't believe what I am going through at the moment. Last night I was very scared wondering what the outcome would be for me. Dear Jesus, please look upon me with Grace and Favour. This journey is now so much about trusting in You. Please guide me God in doing what is necessary for a full recovery.

March 10,

Huge amount of pain during last night, lymph nodes and swelling don't work well together. I am feeling guilty about taking another aspirin, third night in a row. Very angry and pissed off with Chi. He chucked everywhere tonight. Then, I was angry at myself for getting angry. I made up this afternoon by giving him a well needed brush!

Phil's twenty year old cat Chi was at Phil's side always. This cat would have watched more sport in its twenty years than most people, and he would cling onto Phil with his life as he jumped around the house cheering on his favourite team or horse. As much as it often annoyed Phil that he could never sit on the couch without Chi being there, quietly he loved it, and of course loved Chi, as we all did.

March 12,

Confusion reigns, really in two minds about what path to follow for my recovery. Massive pain in my arm last night and my prayers have become desperate pleas: Dear Jesus, please cure me of cancer. Mother Mary, please guide your son to one hundred percent health. Holy Ghost, please enter my body and cleanse me.

At this point Phil was still exercising and on this day, exactly one month before he died, he wrote, "I have had a good day physically with my one armed workout, my fifteen minute walk and half an hour pool work out." This was truly amazing for a man who was so close to facing his own mortality on the twelfth of the following month.

March 13, "Went to the Warriors game with Oscar and Owen. Felt good to get well and build a body like Steven Price. Feeling lost with what direction to take with health."

My sister in law Delwyn was another angel on this journey with Phil and would often assist him with Yoga techniques to ease his breathing. Phil was truly seeing the depth of love others had for him as he wrote on March 14,

> Delwyn has such a heart, and I appreciate this act of love a great deal. It is also interesting for me to take on board that people do love me. Dear God, I need Your guidance with my healing plan. I don't know which path to take. My prayers are there and have become somewhat desperate. Please show me a sign to lead me where You know I should be going in my healing recovery, if this be Your will.

March 15 was the day that I arrived home from my week away. I remember coming through the arrival gates and seeing Phil in his red sweatshirt. I thought he looked well and commented to him about this to which he responded with a nervous, rather sarcastic laugh.

I could not wait to see Phil, I bought him a lot of clothing whilst away, the kind he liked, sports tops and shorts for his gym workouts. This I had hoped would be an incentive for him in his recovery as he loved the gym so much and the camaraderie with his fellow mates there. Phil's journal on that day reads,

> Tanya home, and I appreciate that. I have made a decision to resign from work. I need to put myself first and become selfish. I am the architect of my future.

What astounded me was that he felt this to be an act of selfishness when he was in fact such a selfless man and feeling so unwell.

Two days later was a big day for Phil. Such a proud man, he finally resigned from work, and I was overjoyed by this decision:

Another step in my journey, I have resigned from Progressive effective immediately. Dave Chambers was superb, very understanding of all angles from a humane point of view. He offered unlimited sick leave, but my integrity said no. I couldn't leave that sitting there. I have decided to look after myself for the first time. I cried this morning due to what I feel is a daunting task for Tanya. I told her "If you'd known I was going to get this then you shouldn't have married me." Got what I deserved in terms of a telling off and reassurance that I would be doing the same for her (no doubt!).

The next few days Phil felt very relieved about his decision to resign from work, and this now enabled him to concentrate totally on his recovery. Unfortunately, this took a turn for the worse, and his body began to decline rapidly. He was feeling huge discomfort in his stomach, a terrible bloating and acid feeling, and a burning sensation in his stomach as he would describe it. He was beginning to vomit and all of a sudden began to feel extreme physical discomfort. However, once again he was concerned for me and writes, "Tanya being an angel but now has a cough, so we need to watch that it doesn't develop and move."

Here was this man concerned about a measly cough that I had when his entire system was now being ravaged and poisoned and, unbeknown to us, beginning to shut down. Phil very rarely complained when he was ill. In fact, I would often not hear about an ailment until it was over and the thought of taking even an aspirin to Phil was not a solution.

One of the most difficult visions of Phil during this time would have taken place a few days before Easter when he was still sleeping in the bed with me. His pain was unbearable that night so he got up and sat in the chair in the alcove in our bedroom.

We had two large chairs facing one another which Phil and I would keep as a quiet corner and where much of my journaling would take place. That night Phil got himself up, and I followed. We turned on the lights, and as he sat in the chair I knelt beside him. He looked desperately into my eyes and said, "I did not ever think that my time on this earth would be so short." Hearing these exact words I will never forget, nor will I ever forget the look of despair in his eyes as he spoke them.

In spite of knowing the truth that Phil spoke, what instantly came from me were words of encouragement to him, "Of course you are going to make it, and you will beat this."

My heart however felt as though it had been shredded at that point, beyond repair. He looked at me with his blue eyes, and without saying a word his lingering desperate look into mine said to me, Tanya, I am hearing you, and I want to believe you, but somehow I find it very difficult to at this moment.

All I wanted to do was protect Phil from the emotional pain that he felt at this time. I was trying to raise his fighting spirit, but I felt so totally out of control and powerless over the physical pain that he was enduring at that moment.

Did Phil need to speak to me that night about his imminent death as I knelt beside him, and was it in fact me who could not go there? This I will never know.

Even in the midst of what was now happening to Phil's body he still did not want to worry anyone. He held so much of his distress and discomfort to himself. How grateful I feel for his journal now so I can comprehend on some level what was really happening for this special man as he was preparing himself for his God.

During these days he wrote,

I have come to the journal because I am very pent up! Hot, bothered, agitated, angry, frustrated. Finding it very difficult to release bouts of pain and refuse in my stomach. My dear Jesus, Please Help Me!!

It distressed me to read these words for the first time after Phil had passed away, but that was Phil, not wanting to concern me. This was between Phil and the "big fellow upstairs."

March 25, only eighteen days before Phil passed away, was Good Friday. On this day every year Phil and I would attend Mass at our Parish at three o'clock then head over to mom and dad's for a meal. This Good Friday was different. We sat together in the lounge, Phil in the cream lazy boy chair that we had recently purchased for him and me on the couch. We often spent many hours like this. I would perhaps have the computer on my lap, or in the evenings we would simply sit and be together.

The significance of Easter was always a major part in our lives every year, and we made an effort to attend mass regularly leading up to Easter Sunday. This year Phil both needed and wanted me by his side and I felt the same. Every day, every moment with Phil was now precious. Deeply I knew he would be leaving me soon. Besides, I knew that Phil wanted me to be near as much as possible. Just to know that I was hovering somewhere in the house was all he needed.

On this Good Friday, I read out aloud the Passion of Christ from the Gospel of John in the Bible. Phil said very little. He just sat and listened and upon reading his journal obviously reflected a lot on the significance of this day.

The following evening I did attend the Easter vigil mass and once again, instead of sitting at my usual spot at the front of the church, I sat at the back alongside the statue of Jesus with his arms outstretched. Somehow I was hoping that those outreached arms would be embracing me during the Mass and during the days to follow, as Phil and I carried out His will with grace and courage.

By this stage Phil had surrendered to the fact that he needed some form of pain relief and had only just commenced taking morphine in tablet form, only eighteen days before his death. At the time I was oblivious to his level of his pain, and it was not until Phil had passed away that I realized how extraordinary this was and what he endured on a physical level. His beliefs were that strong, and they kept him away from the medication until this close to his passing.

His journal on this day was painful to read yet beautiful.

I have had two good days. The lesson learnt is to take the pain killers so that the body can start healing at a cellular level. Two days ago I had my first *I don't know if I can make it through* conversation, simply brought about by pain. Once pain envelopes you, you have very little access out of or around. There is no space to allow you to pray, meditate or dream. Today is Good Friday,

Jesus, pain. The Passion of the Christ, Tanya and I read that today. The flashes from the film were evident in my mind. How courageous and brave was our dear Jesus. No pain killers available for Him, just total faith that He was to carry out His Father's will. My dear Jesus, please be my divine Healer.

This was beautiful for me to read and write again as only recently had I watched the movie of the Passion of the Christ. What was very evident for me were Phil's final hours and how brave and courageous he also was.

During the Saturday Easter Vigil Mass I wept constantly due to the grief that my beloved was not there to join in this celebration with me and that this would in fact be our final Easter together.

Easter Sunday, March 27, was a day that we normally spent with family. Phil could not make it out that day so it was just the two of us with the occasional visitors. My cousins Ivan and Vesna called in to see us, and Phil was out of his chair and sitting in the dining room chatting with them. Such a proud man he was, no lazy boy for him when we had guests.

Ivan and Vesna brought many laughs with them that morning. Phil just loved Ivan's roaring laugh and humour, and it often gave Phil the excuse to be loud as well.

One memorable occasion was when we went to their home for one of Vesna's magnificent meals. Phil sat right next to his buddy Ivan and together they polished off a substantial flagon of Ivan's homemade red wine. As a result I had to drive a very cheerful Phil home and often told the story about this very jovial Phil having to be led from our garage into the front gate. However when I turned around there was no Phil.

Phil mistook our front gate for the toilet door inside the house and, to my horror when I did eventually find Phil, here he was watering the palm garden, thinking that he was doing a good thing and rather pleased with himself as he was laughing loudly about it. Ivan and Vesna brought laughs to Phil on that Easter Sunday when he so needed them.

My brother Antoni also came to visit Phil that Easter weekend, and I do remember Phil thoroughly enjoying this visit and being rather moved by it. Antony's pain was evident to me as he struggled to keep his tears to himself when he saw the deterioration in his "brother" Phil. Sadly, this was the last time that Antony and Phil would speak or hug one another. Phil's writings on this Easter Sunday were also beautiful.

Today I learned that Antoni had been upset at seeing me yesterday. He cried after leaving our house and cried with the family around Easter lunch. I felt honored to have this reaction from him. Again it is another example of how I am appreciated in this world. I only wish Antoni had said something to me at home as then I feel we could have both benefited from conversation and found out like brothers how we are doing. I also said to Tanya that maybe the cross that God has me carrying is a catalyst for this family to open up and talk with each other and share love.

I recall Phil saying these words to me that day.
Phil continues,

Ivan and Vesna visited this morning. As usual, loud, excitement in everyday life, another Croatian Cameo! Uncle Bill and Norma also visited with a hair cut for me too. I feel very close to my Uncle Bill and love him like a dad. Norma is a very loving, caring and spiritual soul. I am wondering how long my arm can stay like this. My dear Jesus, please reduce the size of the swelling in my left arm, if this is Your will.

When he was very ill over these days the poor man began to vomit regularly, and it was very painful and vile for him. As this would be happening I remembered saying to him to somehow offer up his pain, which Phil did and would often say the words that Monsignor Cronin repeated to us so often, "Jesus, remember me."

As the days progressed the lymphoedema in his arm was now so bad that much of the day Phil was confined to this chair due to the weight of his arm. He writes,

Feeling very frustrated and agitated tonight. Left arm feels like it is going to explode, and I now have very little movement in it from the back of the shoulder to the tip of my fingers. My mind set hasn't been too bad but I now wonder how long I can keep this up for? My dear Jesus, please help me with some relief in the swelling of my left side, especially my arm. I can only spend the day between lying on bed and resting on my lazy boy. I am reading a book called *Forgiveness and Other Acts of Love*. It has been a good book for me; courage is not a quick fix. I offer my pain and discomfort to You Jesus, especially at this time of Easter.

My own recollections of these days were of absolute exhaustion and busyness. My days were comprised of nursing Phil and doing what I had to do to keep him comfortable. This I believe with every fiber of my soul is the greatest role I have ever played in my life, and in fact, ever will. By this point I was accepting offers from others to bring meals over, and I was very appreciative of it.

The time had come when Phil was not able to sleep in our bed due to the discomfort and was every night in his cream lazy boy, therefore our lounge room also became my bedroom and the couch was now also my bed.

Often I would awaken during the night with pains in my hips due to the discomfort of the couch so when I was sure that Phil was asleep I would go into our bedroom to get some sleep in our bed until the sound of his call would alert me that he was again awake. If Phil was awake, then it was important for me and for him that I was simply beside him.

Being in our bed on my own was extremely sad for me. This would be the time when my mind would be quiet and my fear would arise as I pleaded for the strength to cope with each day and for whatever lie ahead for me on this journey.

As I have mentioned, Phil kept a journal for a little while before his cancer diagnosis, and what it contained were many writings from books he was reading, notes, ideas for management. The journal had a lot of content. However, after he was diagnosed, the content changed, and, in addition to Phil writing about the happenings of his days, his writing became more about his feelings and how he was processing these feelings. His true feelings began to pour out, some of which I am writing in this book—those which I feel are appropriate and sit right for me to share.

As the days progressed his writings altered and began to be prayers and pleas for healing and, finally, a letting go on some level—an acceptance of his fate.

March 29,

A very bad sleep with a lot of pain in my arm. My dear Jesus, please release me from pain. Be my divine healer, if this is Your will. I took my low dose of morphine basically every two hours. However the pain remained. I spent the morning in my lazy boy in and out of sleep. Tanya has had a session with her counselor, and I feel happy about that as she needs to keep her strength up. She is an angel at my side.

As the news of Phil's illness became public knowledge and it ran through the veins of Progressive Enterprises, the emails and letters of support came flooding through immediately. As they did I would build up a contact list of people and began to keep everyone informed of what was happening for Phil, for us both. Phil wanted people to have an update of his condition and this way the ease of bulk emails did take the pressure off me in contacting people.

Some very special emails and words of encouragement came through, many people drawing on their faith and sharing it with us. Thank you all for this encouragement for Phil and myself. Phil often referred to his male friends as brother, and he particularly liked this email from one of his *bothers* from Progressive:

My brother, I am distraught at the news of your health. There seems to be no sense at the indiscriminate nature in which this disease seems to choose its victims. I am left to assume it is only on the basis that the Lord has a grand plan for us all which sometimes leaves mere mortals a little confused.

Although our paths have been somewhat separated over the past few years, the fun times and learning experiences you have, and will continue to partake in with everyone you come into contact with, are cherished.

The thing I think you don't understand is that greatness can only be measured by the lives a person touches, directly or indirectly, and believe me when I say your greatness, love and passion cannot be measured.

The shock and disbelief and pain I am feeling for you and Tanya is tangible evidence of the bond we have built over the years.

Be strong, as I know you are, to conquer the fight you have ahead my friend.

I'm sorry if this note seems somber; it is not intentioned that way.

Yours sincerely,

Warwick "Hurricane" Holmes

SEVEN

Surrender

During the next few days Phil progressively became worse. The acid feeling and swelling in his stomach, the vomiting and lack of appetite, and his change in colour was evidence that his body was slowly shutting down. His legs down to his toes were now both swollen from lymphoedema, and his left arm was now unbearably large, right down to his fingertips.

It felt like a race against a beast that I just could not keep up with. What more was I able to do to keep my love alive. Or was I also to surrender and come to a point of accepting that now my job was simply to keep him as comfortable as I possibly and humanly could, until it was his time to go to God?

The cancer had taken over; this was clearly visible. Unlike other diseases where you become so deathly thin you look as though you will disappear to nothing, Phil was the opposite. Most of his body was swelling by the day. In fact to me he looked rather beautiful as many others also said. He had a beauty around him that was unexplainable. He was beginning to lose weight in his face and his right arm was also becoming thinner. I would often see him glancing over at this arm to see it becoming smaller, those biceps that he worked so hard and bulked up at the gym were now almost gone.

During my silent staring at Phil one evening I recall watching him scratching his head and feeling something on his head. I was not sure what it was, and I was determined to find out. Part of my nursing was to give him a gentle lymphatic massage that Phil's nurse had taught us to do. Later that evening during this massage I deliberately began touching his head and felt that there were lumps now in his head and also under his right armpit.

It was at this moment I recall being able to fully surrender to the fact that my husband was dying, and I said these words to myself, "I cannot keep up. I cannot do anything to save Phil. Please, Lord, at this time, Remember Me."

Whilst assisting Phil with his showering and toweling down, I did my best to not alarm him with the difficulty I had in doing this or seeing what was happening to his body. I kept reaffirming him as to the beauty of his body, of our bodies. I do remember thinking to myself that only a miracle from God could save this man. I could do no more.

During my own surrender my only thoughts were that I had a job to do, and it was to nurse this man as best as I could, to keep him as comfortable as humanly possible. I wanted to keep his life force and spirit up, to provide him with the medication and anything else possible. I wanted to make this journey tolerable for him physically, emotionally and spiritually if I could and as best as I could.

How I functioned I cannot say. All I know was that once again I was in this robotic state doing my best to not allow him to see my despair which at this point was pushed well down. I knew that I had to stay this way until my beloved Phil left this earth and then it would be my time.

April 3, Pope John Paul II died, and Phil mentioned to me that he had gone to heaven. Somehow I felt that Phil was comforted that this Pope, whom he respected so much, was going to be there when he arrived. However when he wrote in his journal on this day, it was clear that he was continuing to fight his way to recovery.

I must keep the love going in meditation. Thank you toxins; you can leave now; you've done the job you needed to do with me. I love that you are leaving me (cancer). Pain means that I am fighting to become well. I am not dying. What has cancer taught me? —I am loved and appreciated. The cancer no longer serves me, and it is OK for it to leave me. I am staying here; the cancer is leaving. I am grateful for what the cancer has taught me—love, appreciation, forgiveness. Hey, I am staying; what do I want to do with this life?

Phil wrote a summary of his day.

Pope John Paul II has gone to heaven. Antoni has had a motor-bike accident. Zel looks smashed. What next? I inform my surrogate son, Oscar, about my Cancer. I cuddle and kiss Smiljan, and I tell him that I love him. Today with Antoni I see the outcome of pain, which is Love.

April 4,
    Pain and discomfort in my stomach has taken its toll; there is not much energy from me. I balled my eyes out as a build-up of not being able to have any contact for wellness with Antoni. My thoughts on what Tanya's going through with me and her brother, my thoughts on Zel with his brother Antoni and brother in law, my thoughts on mom and dad with two sons unwell. I am incapacitated at this moment in time, and it is important that I nurture myself to wellness so I can help others when they are in need. Things built up for Tanya yesterday also. She had a big balling tears breakdown just like things getting too much. I love to see her tears as I know they strengthen her. We both agreed last night that the two days in the hospice that my doctor wants won't happen. I need Tanya and she needs me around at this time

This night I remember vividly: Phil was sitting in his cream lazy boy chair, only a few dim lights were on in the lounge, so there was softness in the room. I was kneeling on the ground by Phil's chair facing him on his right side which was not swollen. I was able reach him here without causing any pain. Holding his hand, I was caressing his fingers. His fingers on this hand were perfect, long slim fingers, piano playing fingers I used to tell him.
    Words were not spoken between us; they were not necessary. We simply looked at one another. I did not want to, but I began to weep quiet

gentle tears. They became heavier and soon there was not a dry spot from these tears that now covered my cheeks, and they began to trickle down my neck and chest.

In the midst of this extreme pain I felt calmness as I looked into Phil's eyes. His body was slowly giving in but his spirit was very much alive. What I saw in him was a beauty that was indescribable at the time. The best way I could now describe it is in one word, and it was love. It felt as though I was gazing at the most beautiful work of art, and nothing was able to distract me from the extraordinary beauty that it was for me in that moment.

These tears I did not want to hide from Phil, I let them flow as it was the only way that I could speak to him at this time. Phil's blue eyes were dry. He was there for me, with such courage. We gazed at one another and with the arm that he was able to move, his right arm, he brushed the hair that was now sticking to my cheeks and wiped my tears. Still no words were spoken. However from my heart I was telling Phil how much pain I felt. I was telling him that I knew he would be leaving me soon, and with his eyes and with the most gentle smile on his face, I knew he was saying to me, "I know Tarn, and it will be OK."

Phil did not want to leave me; I knew that this thought was unbearable for him. So often I reflect on how much more difficult this journey would have been for him had he also to leave his own flesh and blood without a father.

The night of April 6 and April 7 Phil and I spent at a hospice with the intention of stabilizing his medication and providing me with a rest at home. However, nothing would keep me from his side.

On our first night there, Phil was sitting in the lazy boy in the corner of the room, and I was upright in his bed. Suddenly Phil turned to me, looked at me for a moment and said, "Tarn, if it is God's will that I die from this, I am at peace with that; I can accept it. However I don't think that I am going to!"

In spite of those final few words that he added after the "however," deep down I felt an incredible relief to hear him say this. I could not bare the fact that on some level he had not accepted the reality. There was even a feeling of slight excitement for me once hearing it. There was a relief for

me that I did not have to say those words to him, honey, you are dying. I
then knew that deep down in his heart, Phil knew.

My thinking also shifted between a state of denial and knowing that
Phil was deteriorating fast. I still had not fully comprehended the perma-
nence of what Phil's death meant and how final it really was. All I had to
do was to stay strong until then and see him to that point.

Phil wrote an entry on this night giving some detail of where he was
and why.

Tanya again has been fantastic, driving me where I need to go,
caring and raising my fight instinct. She is going to sleep with me
at St Joseph's tonight. Hope to have comfortable evening for both
of us. Dad and mum came around home to do lawns and vac-
uum house. I love them both so much.

Reading this made me sad. I wondered how surprised Phil was that I
would have, and did anything for him at that time, anything to help him
to stay alive, to be comfortable and to have a comfortable death. This came
so naturally to me. I knew that it was what I had to do, and, as traumatic
as the entire journey was, I would do it again in a heartbeat for this man.

The following day, April 7, was Phil's last entry in his journal. He simply detailed content of what had happened during his day and what had
been found during the tests that he had whilst at the hospice. Phil also
kept a separate journal that he commenced on January 11 which he called
his "Gratitude Journal." Its purpose every night was to look for six things
that happened in his day to feel grateful for and, whilst in the midst of his
own terror, to look for what good was happening in his life, which he did,
every night until the final day of his journal writing.

The most beautiful entry he made for me was his final entry of this
journal, April 7. I believe he was writing it as a way of expressing his feelings to me and saying goodbye.

I am grateful for God allowing me to meet and marry my beautiful wife Tanya. She has been so supportive, courageous and in
unconditional love.

Thank you for those words Phil, I would not have had it any other way.

Phil did not want to stay in the Hospice any longer than he had to, and on April 8 after having a foot massage from Michele, his masseuse, Phil left the hospital that afternoon. In spite of his condition and the discomfort from his swollen body, he insisted on not leaving in a wheel chair but to walk out of that place on his own two swollen feet.

Whilst I carried the bags, Michele walked in front of Phil so that he could rest his arm at a ninety degree level on her shoulders. The weight of his arm at this point was far too heavy and painful for Phil to endure. I still marvel at how extraordinary Phil was to do this.

Slowly we got to the car. Phil and I made our way home and into our home at Jervois Road, back into his cream lazy boy chair, just in time to meet his strong desire to watch the funeral of Pope John Paul II. It was very important for Phil to get home for this, and he watched the funeral in its entirety that evening until approximately eleven o'clock.

He was quiet as he watched. Very few words were spoken, however, I recall Phil commenting on the simplicity of the Pope's casket. Rather than having it at a high level, his casket was placed on the ground at the level of his people. Phil liked this.

I would often glance at Phil and wonder what he was feeling that night as he watched this ceremony and wondered if the few words Phil mentioned was some way of giving me instruction on what he wanted at his own funeral.

Once again my parents came over as did Phil's sister Marie and her husband, Neil. I remember it being an evening of busyness—staying busy and on some level having left my own body as I watched this helpless, scared woman *doing,* unable to sit and simply *be.*

Phil's final weekend on this earth was one of confusion and sadness. Some very close friends visited briefly—those who were closely involved with Phil's journey. There were many people whom Phil did not want visiting and some who did not even know of his condition. This was how Phil wanted it. Right from the onset he was clear on his need to keep to his decision. Phil could be rather stubborn on some levels and rightly so. This was one of those times when he was able to say no and mean it, and I respected his *no.*

This was, after all, his journey and his alone. Only Phil could set the scene on how he wanted this final act of his life played out. To this day I am at peace in my heart in respecting Phil's wishes during this time.

During his final Saturday Phil shed tears as he held hands with his friend, both of them knowing what was happening but not wanting to voice that word goodbye, only to say it with their eyes and hearts.

Phil was very tired however he insisted on getting up out of his cream lazy boy chair to see out these close friends who had been on this journey with him. In fact, he walked them outside and stood on our back deck in the sunshine and waved them goodbye. Phil enjoyed the autumn heat on his face for a moment as I stood in the kitchen watching him. As he was returning into the house he stopped at the entrance of the door on the back deck and held onto its side, and I watched in awe as he began doing gentle squats. Up and down he squatted with both swollen legs. Clearly I was astounded, and when I asked him what on earth he was doing, his reply was, "I am getting my legs back into shape Tarn."

At some point during that weekend our counselor and friend David, whom Phil was seeing during his illness, called in to see us. David and Phil became very close and it was he who has continued to be my support during my journey which followed. I hurried myself within the home as they sat together, not as counselor and client but as fellow brothers deeply sharing their feelings, once again without a lot of words spoken.

David read to Phil that day and obviously the most appropriate reading. He shared to me some weeks later that Phil responded and said, "Thank you; I feel better now."

David also shared with me that during the final month of Phil's life, it was he who was in fact learning from Phil.

I too understand what a privilege it is to walk beside someone during the final stage in this life.

The following day Phil was very tired and slept in his chair most of the day. It was a much quieter day. It was the final time I saw and heard Phil laugh, that loud infectious laugh, as I conveyed yet another story of my dad's crazy antics that day.

Deep down Phil believed that he would be going somewhere far greater. Upon reading his journal he was reflecting on and made a list of any regrets that he would have from this life if he did in fact die from cancer. At the end of his brief list he wrote, "I guess I wouldn't have too many regrets. I'd hopefully be with God ready to do battle at his side."

Phil's doctor Rhona was keeping a close watch at this point to ensure that he would get some relief from the continuous agony that he endured from the swelling and to be able to get some sleep during those dark nights.

During those final nights I too would be with him on the couch in the lounge, taking short bursts in my bed when I could hear that the medication had worked and that Phil would be asleep.

I was functioning insanely like a desperate robot, doing whatever I could to keep this man alive, knowing very well that he was slipping away from me as each day passed. It would not be until many months later that I would suffer the fallout from this tumultuous time.

Phil would still shower himself and I would towel him down. The pain in his arm and shoulder was now so unbearable for him that he would need to sit in a swivel chair to rest his arm. I would towel down his body, and he would shave himself with his still functioning right arm.

Some days towards the end Zel would come over and give Phil a treat by shaving him and massaging his face whilst he reclined in his cream lazy boy chair. It was beautiful to see—as these two brothers would share and in their own way were saying goodbye during these moments.

Phil had a courage that I had never witnessed before in my life. I remember thinking to myself during these days as I would towel him down that only a miracle from God could spare him. I even doubted that anything at this point could repair what I was seeing. The thought would quickly sneak in, and just as quickly I would dismiss it as nothing could take me from this state of pure adrenalin. I had a job to do, and I was to keep doing it.

One memory at this time that is still lodged in my mind was when we were in the bathroom and Phil was sitting in his swivel chair. I noticed the look of anguish in those blue eyes as he looked at his reflection and was scanning his body. He then looked up at me with that same desperate glance that I had seen before that night in our bedroom and said, "Look at me Tarn, look at my body."

My heart was crushed as I replied, "Phil you are beautiful."

The most profound words of wisdom then came from Phil that I hold to this day, "This is God showing me that it is not about the physical but all about the spiritual." The only words I could respond with were to agree with him and once again be amazed by the depth of faith that this beautiful man had.

In our lounge to the left of his cream lazy boy chair we had many family photos on the wall, along with a beautiful picture of Jesus which Phil looked at often. It was in fact his favorite image of Jesus. We also had a large piece of green heavy paper and on it together we did a montage of all of the positive feedback we had received from people and occurrences over the past five months to remind us that Phil was being taken care of. In the centre of this montage we placed an early photo of Phil and I, also his favorite.

Phil would often look up at these words of affirmation to remind himself that he was going to make it. This weekend though when he looked in the direction of these photos he was looking at the photo of his deceased mother Moira, and he said to me, "I am now looking how my mother did just before she died." Whilst I did not voice this to him all I could do was look at him and acknowledge with a gentle nod his comment. However inside I thought, yes, honey, you are.

The day before Phil died was Monday, April 11. It was a rather quiet day which I appreciated and we spent the afternoon in front of the TV together, watching a funny DVD I recall. He was very tired and quiet and at this point not eating a lot, only sipping on some milk shakes which he enjoyed.

Thankfully I only left his side for a few moments that day to go to the store across the road to get some supplies. I too was not eating a great deal by this time and what was consumed was rapidly being burnt off by the amount of physical and emotional energy that my body was using. I was getting thinner, however I did not care as I too wanted to die and perhaps this was one way that I could.

That evening I felt a physical exhaustion like I had not felt before. All I wanted to do was sleep, but nothing at this point would keep me in that restful state for more than a couple of hours at a time. My nerves were at breaking point, my days were long and tiring, however there was no way that I would leave Phil's side as this was where I knew I had to remain.

Once I was sure that Phil was asleep in his cream lazy boy chair I went into my bed to rest, unaware that this would be the last night I would tend to Phil's needs in our home in Jervois Road. I felt very lonely going into that room that night. It no longer felt like our bedroom as I lay there alone. As my thoughts came the desperation I felt was different somehow. Perhaps on some level I knew what was awaiting me the following day.

All I knew to do was to surrender myself to God and ask to be carried at this time, to give me the physical energy to get through yet another day. Even though I knew that Phil was only in the room next door a feeling of loneliness surrounded me. I cried and before I knew it only a few hours later I was awake, sensing somehow that Phil too was awake. When I would first awaken there would be a few seconds of reprieve from the nightmare as I would forget, but then reality came. Oh how many times I simply did not want to awaken.

That night I was up during the night with Phil a few times then back again into my bed when he settled. I was awakened at four o'clock to Phil calling out to me. My recollection of this call was significant for me as I remember feeling for the first time that physically I could not go on much longer. Once Phil was settled again, I managed to sleep again for a short while until seven o'clock on April 12 when I awoke to Phil calling, "Tanya."

EIGHT

April 12, 2005

On April 12, 2005 Phil was scheduled to have a CT scan to see the extent of his cancer, however, upon awaking that morning, Phil was distressed and said to me that he did not feel he could make this appointment. I knew for Phil to cancel this he was feeling very bad and that he had surrendered even more.

Phil was not well, he had taken a turn for the worse during the night, so I phoned his doctor Rhona and she arrived within the hour at approximately eight o'clock. Phil had a fever. His skin was clammy, and Rhona informed us that he would need to go to hospital for antibiotics as it was her suspicion that he was now suffering from an infection, which subsequently proved to be correct.

Rhona stayed with Phil and myself awhile once she had organized the hospital and ambulance. I quickly began moving around the house and packing overnight gear for us both. I once again returned to the robotic state—a state that I had now mastered and seemed somewhat comfortable in.

During this time Rhona sat with Phil and asked him how the hospice visit went for him. He replied, "not very good actually Rhona, those hospice nurses aren't very experienced are they!" Bless him, both Rhona and I looked at one another with a gentle smile. We both found this rather funny actually, but Phil was pretty serious when making this statement. To him the only nurse who knew how to look after him properly was his wife Tanya.

April 12, a Tuesday, was the day that Phil was to close his final act, and on that morning he showered himself and as usual I toweled him down. How remarkably strong he was, both physically and in spirit. This too was the final time that this ritual of ours would take place.

The ambulance arrived on time at 9.45 A.M., and I could tell by the look on the faces of the ambulance attendants that they felt this was going to be one large ask to get Phil onto the stretcher. Not only was Phil a tall man, at this stage his body was very swollen so he would have been extremely heavy.

Phil was a man of such dignity, to surrender himself and allow others to lift him onto this stretcher was telling me that he no longer had it in him to manage with his own body in spite of the fact that he had showered himself earlier that morning. The body that he took so much pride in and worked so hard at keeping in shape, the body he loved so much was now taking control of him and he was now surrendering to it.

Again I was functioning on pure adrenalin. The tiredness from the night before was gone as I gathered all of the items that we needed for the hospital visit, not really knowing for how long. Once this was done, and standing at the entrance of our lounge with bag in hand, I distinctly recall seeing the beauty of the sun streaming through our stain glassed window and onto Phil as he was being placed on the stretcher.

That little voice inside, the one I grew to know and at times despise, told me that this would be the last time that I would have Phil in our home alive. I did not dismiss the voice at this time. I knew that he was now being taken away for the absolute final stage of his journey and that someday soon, this journey of Phil's would be complete.

For a moment the part of me that remained in denial wanted to scream to the ambulance officers not to take him from his cream lazy boy chair, thinking that somehow if Phil remained at home he would not die, that he would remain with me forever and no matter what state he was in it was fine with me. There was however the part of me that had completely surrendered and had no voice left to scream, no tears to cry, just a knowing that my act was not quite complete. For how long I was not sure. What I did know was to continue to stay strong for Phil, and soon it would be my time to fall apart.

Phil was being carried from our home on a stretcher, carried out onto the main road where the ambulance was parked. He did not have the energy to walk out there on his own, as he did only five days earlier from the hospice.

I rode with Phil in the ambulance answering all of the questions asked by the attendant, being incredibly precise about his condition, the medication he was on, times and test results. You name it; I answered it. I was in my fight mode, no flight for me at this time as clearly the adrenalin was fully operating.

Phil lay there now with an oxygen mask on to assist his breathing, totally trusting in nurse Tanya as I sat slightly behind him, gently caressing his head to let him know that I was there.

There was such a vast difference to the man whom I recall merely six weeks earlier wanted to remain independent and do as much for himself as he could. Upon my return from overseas, within hours in fact, I noticed that Phil had let go and in his own way said, Tarn, I need you to take care of me now.

Once we arrived at the acute assessment ward at Auckland Hospital there was urgency in my voice as I said, "Please, take care of him for me and help me." There was a feeling of relief for me as I handed over the physical task of taking care of Phil to someone else. It was too much for me—both physically and emotionally I could do no more.

As we waited a few moments for Phil to be admitted, once again he was asked a familiar question by the nurse admitting him, "You remind me of someone, but I cannot think of whom." To put her out of her misery I rather promptly replied as I knew that they were referring to Christopher Reeve, the Superman actor who was crippled in a horse riding accident and had recently died himself. I know her intentions were kind, but I did not want precious moments wasted when all I really wanted them to do was ease the load upon us both at this time. Phil did look very much like Christopher Reeve, and in fact a friend of my mother's once asked why she had a photo of Superman on her mantle piece. Phil was my superman, and, even as he lay there helpless, he still was.

News had travelled very fast about Phil now being in the hospital, and for so many it was a shock as they were not aware how close he actually was to the end of his time. Many family members were still unaware that he had cancer, and this was how Phil wanted it.

For the first few hours it was just the two of us as doctors and nurses attended to Phil, asked more questions, took x-rays, looked for veins in which to place the IV drip for his antibiotics and attached monitors to him. These monitors confirmed my reality that my husband Philip was slipping away, and it baffled me that this man was still fighting to the degree that he was, considering what those numbers read.

As I sat there listening to the doctors, trying to understand them, it was clear that Phil did have a severe infection which they would attempt to fight with antibiotics. However all of his major organs were now slowly closing down. The simple fact was that Phil's body was barely alive; however his fighting spirit was still very much with us and this was the only reason that he was still with us.

One of the many reasons that Phil was so loved by everyone was because he placed no human ahead of another. He gave as much time to the trolley boy at the supermarket as he did to his superiors. Phil always made an effort to know people by their first names and refer to them as so, no matter how little he knew them. Yes on the final day of his life he continued with this same respect, and for every nurse or doctor that tended to him that day he asked for their first name and respectfully used it.

Phil was in fact rather comical on this day and made some rather funny comments. I am not sure if it was simply his usual dry sense of humour or whether he was in some euphoric state due to his condition. He certainly was very lucid and not pumped up with pain killers at this point, so I believe it was simply Phil acting out.

One young doctor came in and asked Phil how he was feeling and with a wide smile his response was, "great, it is the best day of my life!"

At approximately midday a senior doctor came in followed by his group of young colleagues. I do not remember his name but surely Phil would have. He had greying hair, a grey beard and glasses, and at that instant he reminded me of the movie director Steven Spielberg. Very directly he asked Phil what his understanding of his condition was. Phil replied in the most positive way that he could, inferring that he was hoping to make it out of there rather soon.

My chest tightened as instinctively I knew that the words about to be spoken from this man would be earth shattering for us both, and they were. For the first time since Phil's diagnosis five months earlier we were told that Phil was going to die and very soon in fact.

No one had ever used the d word before with us; it was as if every doctor and specialist with whom we had contact somehow knew not to. In fact it took me many months after Phil's death before I could utter this word myself.

This was perfect for Phil's journey as never did he want to be told that this cancer would eventually take him from this life. He needed to hear only positive things to assist him in his recovery. Upon hearing these words once again the nausea and trembling began in my body. The horror, the truth, this fact was voiced; my husband was dying. This doctor's exact words were that "You will not be leaving this hospital."

Phil's body was now being ravaged by an infection that was spreading through his body, and it was doubtful that any antibiotic would stop it. All of his major organs were failing, his blood pressure was barely registering and soon my husband of only eight years would leave me.

Upon hearing these words Phil looked at me like a frightened young boy needing comfort that perhaps what he heard was not correct. No words were spoken, however his big blue eyes said to me, "Did you hear what he said Tarn? I am actually going to die."

We were left alone to assimilate the avalanche we had just been hit with. I moved closer to Phil to sit on his bed to his right. I held his hand. There were no tears. I just wanted to be with him to comfort him. He wanted reassurance that the decisions he had made were right, and I told him that everything he had done was perfect, and there was now nothing for him to fear. All we needed to do was to continue to trust in our God and His will for us both. What I recall was an unbearable sadness that I felt for Phil as he lay there now helpless and on some level hopeless. My heart bled for Phil and whatever it was that he may have been feeling at that time. I feel this same pain now as I write.

It was at this moment that Phil said to me "Tarn, don't forget to bring in my journal tomorrow, because this will be good for my book." This was how passionate Phil felt about needing to tell about his journey and why

I feel deeply in my heart that I have Phil's blessing in sharing our story—the one though which we both wanted to have a far different ending.

Upon leaving our home that morning as usual I packed our statue of the Virgin Mary and the picture of the Jesus which Phil so loved. I placed this picture at the end of Phil's bed where he could clearly see it. Together we looked at these treasures of ours during the remainder of that day simply letting go, surrendering to what was now imminent.

Whilst Phil was being attended to by the doctors I found a bathroom and phoned his sister Marie, my brother Zel and my parents informing them the best I could of what we had just been told. Without speaking too loudly I was trying to tell my mother that Phil was dying, but she did not comprehend what I was trying to tell her, so I repeated it to her in Croatian. It was when I heard her erupt with tears and anguish did I know she had finally understood. In spite of her outburst of grief this still did not bring on my own tears. I did not allow them to come as I had a job to do here, and so I thought not to disturb what I have to do for my husband right now.

Zel arrived soon after and sat at the other side of Phil's bed. He barely spoke. The look of despair on his face said it all, and this vision is still imprinted in my memory. Still I had not cried. I could not, and I would not.

One clear recollection of those moments was Phil saying to me, "The doctor said that I only had a few months to live." Gently I held his hand and responded back to him, "Honey that is not what the doctor said," I could not say much more as we were not informed of exactly how long he had, but I knew that it was not a matter of months.

When this beautiful young female doctor returned, and once again Phil knew her by name, I asked her how much time Phil actually had and what we were to expect over the next few days or weeks. In her quiet voice she said that the infection could not be stopped, that it was too aggressive, that his organs would slowly begin to completely shut down, that Phil would eventually fall into a coma and within two or three days he would be gone. "Two or three days," I panicked inside yet appeared calm. I have so little time with him, I thought, yet still there were no tears. Immediately I saw horror in Phil's face as he looked at me once again needing reassurance from me. He even repeated the word, *coma,* as if to say, like hell am I going into a coma.

At one point whilst we were in this ward Phil and I were alone together, and as I was sitting on the end of his bed, he was talking to me about us going on a cruise again. He was "going to eat Birscha Muesli for breakfast and sit on the beach and love his wife"! Once again he was rather humorous as he told me in detail of this adventure.

Later that afternoon Phil was moved into a room on his own and soon immediate family began arriving to see him and provide support to us both but mainly to say goodbye to their brother, son-in-law and friend.

Delwyn was the first to arrive, and my most vivid memory of our time together was that Phil wanted the four of us to hold hands which we did––Zel was to Phil's right, I was on Phil's left, and Delwyn was next to me. It was at this moment when my gentle tears came. In fact only Phil had dry eyes.

The three of us wept as Phil very lucidly spoke to Zel and Delwyn and asked them to look after his girl. I allowed my tears to come as Phil voiced and accepted his fate in the presence of someone else. Through his words to Zel and Delwyn he was in fact saying to me, Tarn, I know that I am dying. Not wanting ever to lose my love, I asked Phil to wait for me when he arrived in heaven, and he said that he would. I hoped that I would be there with him soon.

Soon Monsignor Cronin arrived. He must have known the urgency as it was peak hour traffic, and the rain was pouring down outside. He gave us all communion and gave Phil his final blessing. Phil responded to Mons with a "Thank you," and "God bless you Father," and Father replied to him, "And God bless you also."

My brother Nick had arrived and sat on the bed with Phil for some time holding his hand. Even this sad time did not stop the humour which often occurred between them both as Phil once again asked Nick to stop smoking!

My parents arrived and Phil said special words to them both, telling them how much he loved them. He treated them like his parents, and "Philipi" as dad often affectionately called him was their fourth son. Mom asked Phil if he had eaten any dinner, and Phil's response was, "Not tonight mom, but if I am feeling better in the morning then I will have some break-fast." This was Phil's way of letting mom know that he would be fine, and it was these words my mother held onto. To her this meant that Phil would make it through the night and perhaps even get better soon.

My brother Antoni had only just that day been released from hospital after the serious motorbike accident he had the week before, so he did not get the chance to say goodbye to Phil in person.

What we can all remember about Phil during the early evening of April 12 were his blue eyes. They seemed even brighter than usual somehow as he gazed at me constantly as I nervously moved across the room, his blue eyes following my every move. Mom noticed how he was watching me and mentioned to me that I should stand at the end of his bed so that he could see me and not have to turn his head as I moved around him, which I did.

On this day Phil radiated love. He radiated perfection, just as we all are when we are born into this life. This was who Phil had become just before he was to leave this life. He was in a state of pure love, and we all noticed this about him as he lay watching.

During the final weeks of his life Phil began telling everybody that he loved them, and on this his final night he was doing the same with those big blue radiating eyes.

Soon everyone had left, and, for a short time between approximately five thirty and six o'clock that evening, Phil and I were alone in this room. As I was sitting over him on the bed gently stroking his head and looking into his eyes, he said something to me that we would always remind each other of often during his illness, "Tarn, if you truly believe then miracles do happen." Phil did not want to leave me, and by saying these words to me only five hours before he passed away I realized that he was still try-ing to protect me, to instill in me some hope and to somehow ease my pain. "Yes they do honey," I responded to him with a very quiet voice.

During this brief time Phil was very lucid, and we shared beautiful words together, no tears, just love. I told him that the ten years we had together were the best in my life and that I would not have changed any-thing.

Phil's big sister Marie, her husband Neil and daughter Jessica arrived soon after and spent time with their brother Phil. Jessica, but a teenager, was very brave to be with her Uncle Phil during this time but had to leave the room. Together we sat on the floor outside as she wept. I knew that Phil would have been proud of her strength.

Soon after Phil was then moved onto the seventh floor of the hospital, and he was happy about this. To us seven was God's number and he commented to me about this as I walked alongside the bed as he was being taken there. For Phil any sign that God was present was a good sign, and for him this was a sign.

The only recollection I have of the next two hours was of Phil's brother Paul arriving, and once again Zel arrived with his young son Xavier who also bravely wanted to say goodbye to his Uncle Phil. Phil had time alone with his family and they had left by about eight o'clock. He was tired, and it was now time for us to be alone again.

My bed for the night was to be a mattress in the corner of his room on the seventh floor by the window. I placed the statue of Our Lady on a shelf on a wall so that it was visible to him, and I placed his favourite image of Jesus at the end of his bed so that Phil could also see this clearly. The lights in the room were dimmed. Phil was lying down with his upper body slightly elevated. He had an oxygen mask on to assist him with his breathing, which at this point was becoming more difficult for him.

My friend Catherine was to come in and get keys to our home to stay the night and look after the three cats. She arrived at around eight thirty that evening, and when she walked into the room Phil smiled and said to her, "Look, here is my other angel." Catherine did not stay long. I remembered her strength and composure as she walked in. She was aware that Phil was feeling anxious and assisted him to calm down his breathing somewhat. She took the keys, reassured Phil, kissed him and waltzed out as graciously as she had waltzed in but a few minutes earlier.

The next two and a half hours, one hundred and fifty minutes, were the final moments that I would spend with my husband Phil, and, apart from the occasional visit from the nurses, it was just the two of us. I sat myself down next to his bed and placed my hands on his very thin right arm. Breathing was becoming difficult for him at this point. It pained me as I felt so powerless—just as powerless I had been during this entire five month journey which, for Phil, was soon to end.

We spoke a lot during those one hundred and fifty minutes. I wanted to reassure him that he would be alright, that there was nothing for him to fear. Once again Phil spoke of our cruise and where we would go on our next one. Whilst he spoke I remember thinking to myself how perfect it was that we went on our Caribbean cruise back in November. I realized then how much it meant to him and how those memories were so deeply embedded into his soul. He seemed to be in some euphoric state, once again funny at times. He understood everything that I said to him and responded to me as only Phil knew how.

Soon I came to realize that I was to remain at Phil's bedside for the night. The mattress that I had made for myself in the corner of the room would not be used. There was a deep knowing to stay up and remain awake by Phil's side on this night.

Holding his right arm, I prayed the Rosary so that he could hear, and he listened and breathed. Then I prayed the Divine Mercy Chaplet again so that he could hear, and he listened and breathed. No matter what, I knew to keep praying. This gave Phil great comfort and calmed him as it did also for me.

My peace and strength was unexplainable at that time, and there was this deep knowing within of what I had to do during Phil's final act. The most meaningful task that I would ever accomplish in my life was soon to be completed.

Every now and then Phil would raise his head and look up to see the picture of Jesus that was upright at the end of his bed. He was alert, and I would ask him if he could see the image to which Phil replied, "Yeah, He is my mate." His reply was in the funny way that Phil often joked around; it was perfect.

Suddenly I developed an even deeper sense that Phil would soon leave me, that evening in fact. He would not wait for that two or three days as the young doctor predicted. He would be gone sooner. Like I said, blow the coma. I just knew.

The other thing I knew was that I was alone with Phil and this was how I wanted it to remain—he in my arms, just the two of us, until he left. I would remain awake with him, I would not sleep, and I would simply be with him one last time. Whilst this time would be the most traumatic that I would ever experience in my life, somehow the trauma was minimized by the incredible peace that was surrounding me.

During Phil's final forty five minutes, I told him that I would pray for him every day for the rest of my life. He responded by saying to me that he would now be *my* angel. He said that he would always take care of me and that when I looked up to the stars that he would always be there.

My heart was at peace when at one point during this final hour of Phil's life I felt that he had accepted his fate, that he was now ready to surrender. It was when he raised his head and looked up again at this image of Jesus at the end of the bed. He then softly laid his head back onto the pillow, turned his head towards me and after a few seconds quietly and calmly said to me, "Tarn, whatever He wants."

"Yes honey, whatever He wants," was my response. This was when Phil and I, together, accepted that soon he would leave me and go into his heavenly Father's arms.

Phil continued to have assistance with his breathing for most of our time together, and at one point I removed the oxygen mask and kissed his lips three times, and he responded by kissing me back. For many months after his death, when I would kiss his photo goodnight, I could still feel those three kisses, our final kisses, which I remembered as clearly as on that night. He enjoyed those kisses.

This time was just for Phil and me. It was for us and us alone, and I did not want anyone else present. As the end drew closer I knew that he was ready and a part of me was too. The pain of watching his breathing was just tearing my heart out, yet there was no way I could relieve him of this discomfort. All I knew was to sit and pray. This trial was too much for me. "Please Lord, help me," I continued to ask.

Whilst I did not want to part with Phil, I wanted this discomfort for him to end—to let him go so that he could be in paradise with his mate Jesus whom I knew was waiting for him. I did not want Phil to fear. I kept telling him that Jesus was with us and that he would be all right. Whilst it was difficult to utter these words I knew that I had to for him, so I said, "Honey you go now; it is alright. I will be alright." I held him in my arms, and I continued to tell him that I loved him and that I would be alright and so would he. After looking at me continuously my dearly beloved turned his head slightly away to the left and closed those luminous blue eyes that radiated perfect love. As soon as he released his final breath, there were still no tears for me. I prayed the Our Father, the Hail Mary and the Glory Be as one final assurance that Phil was making his way into His Father's arms.

At approximately 11.10 P.M. on April 12, 2005 Philip Joseph Morrow passed away in my arms. I am not sure how much time passed. My Philip was safely on his way to greater things. His journey was over now; mine had just begun.

I held onto him in stunned silence, continuing to stare at him and surprisingly calm. It felt like a nightmare and that in the morning when I awoke Phil would still be with me. I made phone calls to Phil's sister Marie and Zel. I clearly recall Zel's surprise as he quietly said, "He died?" Marie and Neil, as most people, were very surprised that Phil had passed away so quickly, and she told me that they both sat up in bed in total shock. It was not surprising for me that Phil chose to leave so soon. He was a proud man and lying helpless in that hospital would not be what he wanted. He had completed his final act with dignity.

I made a couple of phone calls to appropriate people knowing that by the time the sun had arisen the following morning the word of Phil's passing would have already been sent around Auckland, as it had. There would have been many a tear shed that night.

In silence I continued to simply sit with Phil looking at his face. My next memory was glancing up as Zel and Delwyn arrived and hearing Delwyn's soft voice as she said "Oh Phil." Still surprisingly calm I continued to hold him not wanting to let him go. Phil's brother Paul also came to the hospital for a short while that night to see his brother that one last time.

To leave Phil's side was not an option for me. The nurses came in to prepare his body to be taken away, but my task still did not feel complete, and I needed to do this. It was me who had to bathe Phil's body one last time and prepare him before they took him away. For how many months had I watched his body, watched it change, washed him, dried him and wiped him down including that evening when he was burning up with a temperature. To bathe Phil one final time was as natural as bathing myself, and I would not have wanted it any other way. I know that Phil would have wanted this. Such a proud man, only his nurse Tanya would have been able to do it as well as he wanted.

Eventually we enclosed Phil's body into something white. I do not recall what it was. Now I felt that for me all was completed, and, as much as I wanted to remain, Phil would be gone, and there would be an empty room. There was now nothing for me to stay for.

It was close to three o'clock in the morning and time for me to leave the hospital with Zel and Delwyn and without my husband Philip. The walk out of the hospital building seemed to go on for eternity. It felt very claustrophobic for me whilst Zel led the way, and Delwyn held me as we made our way out. It was not until I started to leave the building and walk out onto the street in the cool early morning air did the realization come to me of what had happened. I had just witnessed Phil take his final breath. He was gone.

As the cool morning autumn air hit my face, the grief hit me as sharply; I collapsed into a physical grief that I had never experienced in my life. I was leaving now without Phil, just as I knew that I eventually would. This was now real, and I was leaving his body behind.

What I wanted to do was go back to that room on the seventh floor in the hope that Phil would still be there, alive, that this did not in fact happen to me that evening. It could not have.

Delwyn called Zel to help her as she could not keep me upright. My wailing was loud, and in the early hours of the morning it echoed through the quiet Auckland streets, but this did not matter. I knew now that Phil could not hear me, and I had nothing in me to stop this pain and anguish from literally exploding from my heart.

Zel slept in the bed with me that night. He sat upright and read awhile, and I did sleep awhile. The darkness that surrounded me when I did awake at around six o'clock was horrific, and I had wished that I did not awaken at all.

Delwyn came into the room and sat on my bed. I needed her then. I needed her to hold me. I needed to be hugged, and I needed to be mothered. I was exhausted and in pain, and it was Delwyn who provided me with what I needed at that time.

I want to conclude this story of Phil's journey with a final farewell which was written for him from the staff at one of the stores when he was transferred from the role of Store Manager to Area Manager in the Waikato district.

Phil would often write a poem for staff members if ever there was a significant occasion to celebrate, so his staff this time wrote him a poem and had it beautifully framed.

They commented on so many of the things that made Phil so unique, his bad spelling, his driving at the speed limit, his dislike of the computer and, of course, his integrity and the level of respect that he so rightly deserved.

For the Boss

It's the end of an era
We're losing the Boss
With most Store Managers
It's no great loss
But it's different with you Phil
Everyone cares
With cries of "we'll miss him"
Even Pat shed some tears

Such an imposing figure
With that deep manly voice
Why leave us at Westgate
When we're the "Right Choice"

You've always inspired us
With your "Thought of the Day"
But where is the pay raise
Questions Pam Hay

You've shouted us feasts
And dinners so swell

We were just coming to terms
With the odd way you spell

We've gone where you've led us
Your direction was right
But when it comes to the Waikato
Your direction is shite

Your flash new car
Comes with air con
But without G.P.S.
You won't know where you've gone

Now an Area Manager
With your own PC
You'll have to learn how to use it
Or what use will it be?

Good luck with your new role
We wish you every success
And thanks for the party invite
But what's the bloody address

It's now time to say goodbye
To Mr. Philip Morrow
We bid you good luck and farewell
With our hearts full of sorrow

PART TWO

My Journey

NINE

The Final Farewell

It was now Wednesday morning, and I went back to our home early to prepare for Phil's return. Logically I knew that in the simple casket I had chosen, it would be only his body but on some level I was also hoping that Phil would come home to me fully alive.

I was in a slight euphoric state and operating in a state of shock and functioning quite well. I believe that my excitement was at the thought of Phil coming home to me.

The funeral director, Jo, arrived that morning, and we commenced making arrangements at the dining room table whilst others were busily working around me in the house, also preparing for Phil's return. Only immediate family and a handful of close friends were with me that day as they cleaned, answered phone calls and began managing the barrage of flowers that began to arrive.

One of the first things I did that morning was to send out an email to all of those people who were being updated on Phil's condition. Many already knew having been part of the telephone tree that commenced shortly after his death not even twelve hours earlier. For others this email was how they found out about Phil's passing and to receive it was devastating for them.

My email to everyone at 9.02 A.M. that morning read:

Hi there All.…..
For those of you who do not know, my precious Phil passed away
last night April 12 at 11.11 P.M.
He was peaceful, lucid and was ready to go.
Thank you all so much for your prayers and kindness towards
Phil and myself during this journey of his……
All my Love.…..
From Tanya and I know also from Phil.…

Our parish priest Monsignor Cronin came to visit me early that morning and as we sat I shared with him some of Phil's final words. Mons comforted me and encouraged me to now pray to Phil—that he was now with
God and would intercede on my behalf. I clearly remembered these words
and began to pray to Phil immediately. This is something that I do to this
day, asking him for guidance in so many areas of my life. Even in writing
this book I have asked for my words to flow.

In my euphoric state that morning it was clear that my thinking was
not rational as a part of me was excited that Phil would be returning home
soon, and I could not wait. The hours passed and afternoon came. Then
early evening came and still there was no Phil, and at eight o'clock we were
still waiting. As per Jo's instructions I had arranged for there to be many
strong men around to bring Phil's casket into our home as he was rather
heavy.

By that evening I had slept possibly eight hours in the last three days,
and even my exhaustion did not dull the excitement I felt about seeing
Phil again although the wait was becoming difficult for me.

The call came from Jo at approximately eight thirty in the evening. Zel
took it, and she informed him that they were not ready to bring Phil home
yet. "No, he must come," I cried, "I want him back," I could not wait any
longer; just bring him home.

I was sitting next to Zel at the dining room table, and when he placed
the phone down he faced me and held my hands as I sobbed from the dis-

appointment of not seeing Phil that night. Zel told me in a very gentle quiet voice that Phil would not be coming home alive. It was simply his body and that Phil was now in Heaven with God.

This I did not want to hear, rationally I knew it, but the words were excruciating for me. I continued to shed the tears that so desperately needed to be released from the long wait during the day. Slowly I glanced around at others in the room wanting to see some signs of support. No matter in which direction I looked, all I saw were more tears from the room full of people who were there watching this scene.

The truth was that Phil was home but not the home that I wanted him to return to. Delwyn comforted me as only she knew how to and told me that perhaps this was Phil's way of giving me a night's rest. Perhaps tonight I needed to sleep, and if he returned I would not have wanted to leave his side. She was right and that night with the help of medication I slept.

The following morning on April 14, Phil's simple casket returned to our home at around ten o'clock, and once again my helpers were there to assist. Standing at the entrance to my home I watched the boys who all looked very strained as they brought the heavy casket inside. I waited anxiously and was excited knowing I was to see my Phil again.

We placed Phil's casket in the centre of the alcove in our lounge with the beautiful stained glass windows which he so loved above his head. Pillows were placed around the casket, and by the end of that first day the bay window where people could sit was covered with the most beautiful array of flowers. To the left of Phil's casket was the large cream lazy boy recliner chair on which he spent most of the final two weeks of his life. It was now empty.

His casket was placed on the floor, and I stood above it anxiously as each of the screws of the lid were turned. One by one they were removed, and when the lid of the casket was gently lifted I saw a body. It was Phil's––his shell only, and in that instant I knew that it was not Phil in the form that I had hoped he would return. My heart sank somewhat. When I saw him I smiled and said, "Oh Phil this is not you; you have gone." I felt an immediate peace in my heart and an acceptance that Phil was not returning home. He was in a far greater place, and this was simply the physical body which once held his soul.

During the following three days our home was open to those who wished to come to pay their respects to Phil, to be with him in this way one more time. Phil and I had not discussed funeral arrangements at all. Instinctively I just knew what to do, what I believe Phil would have wanted for his final farewell.

Having Phil in our home was something I believe he wanted as we had often talked about what a beautiful ritual this was. I felt it was the right thing to do for others and especially for myself as it enabled me slowly to let go of the physical of Phil.

During those three days as Phil lay there in our lounge, the skies were brilliant blue, and the days were warm as friends, family and acquaintances came to pay their final respects. My home was very busy and at times there were queues of people outside on our deck enjoying the beautiful Autumn days as they waited to say goodbye to their *brother* Phil.

At night I slept on the floor or the couch in the lounge with his casket with either Catherine or Delwyn at my side. All three cats also slept with us. At one point during the night Delwyn awoke needing a drink from her glass of water only to disturb Phil's twenty year old cat Chi having a drink first! Things like this made us laugh. I am sure Phil was also laughing.

Chi sat on a large chair next to Phil's casket for the entire three days that Phil was there. He rarely moved or ate. He became thinner, and in his own way grieved as he too was letting go of his master. Our second cat Rudi who was also jet black did not want to come in too close when we were there. He looked in from a distance and would simply sit at the entrance of the lounge and just observe. I did catch him on occasion coming in to smell Phil and perhaps say his goodbye also.

Fergus on the other hand was a different story. He was our grey tabby stray who joined the household about eighteen months earlier and whom Phil and I just adored. He had the personality of a comedian and constantly needed to be the centre of attention. Well Fergus became quite a pest during these days as many a time he thought it would be a good idea to hop in the casket with his dad and see what was happening, have a sniff around and perhaps even have a nap in there. Often I had to haul him out. Phil would have found this very amusing!

These three days were very busy and on some level I had disassociated from the reality of the situation. It felt as though I was having an out-of-body experience, observing myself from afar, all of the people coming and going, people holding others in their grief and putting my own aside. Sometimes your conscious mind can only take so much, and I believe that I had reached my limit in observing Phil's final breaths. All I had to do was get through the next few days until the funeral was over, and then my time of grieving would come, when I was silent and alone.

There were many items placed by all into Phil's casket such as poems, small gifts, and even the horse racing guide went in there. With Phil being such an avid horse follower he would have liked this. In addition to his mother's rosary beads, I placed a photo in Phil's casket, his favourite one of the two of us which was taken very early during our relationship.

During the late afternoon on Friday, the day before Phil's funeral, I excused myself from guests and went to rest on my bed wanting to sleep––needing to sleep in fact. However at that point I was over tired and no rest came. I had decided to give the eulogy at the funeral the following day. It was then that I reached over and began to write.

My thoughts at the time were, how I could write anything now in this state, so I simply asked my angel Phil to direct my words, to show me what it was that I needed to say, and my words just flowed, my pen did not stop writing until I completed what I needed to say. That Friday night before Phil's final farewell, we had a final gathering at our home for family and very close friends to be together with Phil and to pray for him. It was a beautiful scene in our lounge which by then was laden with bouquets of flowers all around and a scent that was breath taking. The lights were dimmed. We all sat around the edge of the room, and I knelt beside Phil to the left of the casket as Monsignor Cronin led us all in the Rosary, something which I believe that Phil would have loved. At the end of each decade Father recited the prayer "Eternal rest grant to him Oh Lord, and may perpetual light shine upon him. May he rest in peace." This prayer I recite every day for Phil

Fergus decided during the Rosary that everyone must have gathered to visit him and made his grand entrance and decided to perform to ensure that he remained the centre of attention with everyone. Phil would have laughed at this!

This would be the final night that Phil lay in our home so once again the girls and I all slept around his open casket with the cats no doubt. We all had our own special time with Phil before the time came for him to be taken away in the morning.

Our minds are such incredible machines, being aware of what it can and cannot cope with as I have the strangest recollections of the morning of the funeral.

I recall the girls making me the largest thick shake to provide me with some energy for what lay ahead that day. I remember looking at myself in the mirror whilst doing my hair and noticing for the first time how thin my arms had become. I remember the big burly men as they had arrived to carry Phil from our home. I remember the hot autumn sun that day. I remember seeing from the kitchen window the hearse arriving and parking on the foot path of the side street with its back hatch door open ready to receive the casket with my beloved Phil inside. That is all I remember. To this day I cannot recall how Phil's casket made its way to the hearse, a sight which I knew would be too much for me to bare on this day. This day I already had too much to deal with. This was the final day which I knew I had to be strong for Phil. Just one more day, I thought.

My next recollection was the slow drive to the church that morning and sitting in the front seat of the hearse with Jo I asked her if it was normal that I felt so controlled and together. She assured me that yes, it was very common with widows and that I was probably in shock. My immediate thoughts were that's good, long may it last as this state was manageable for me.

Once at the church Jo mentioned to me that Phil's casket was very heavy, and, whilst I had made the request for him to be carried on the shoulders of the pall bearers, it would probably prove to be very difficult for them. My very graceful reply to Jo was that I understood this fact but that it was still my desire that Phil be carried into the church on the shoulders of the pall bearers, as he so rightly deserved. Jo obliged.

Subsequently my brother Zel did say to me that Phil was "bloody heavy," and I thought to myself, yes. I am sure that Phil would have been having a good old laugh about that. He was often referred to as hollow legs by my brothers because of his ability to eat vast amounts of food and yet still remain so lean!

Approximately seven hundred or more people attended Phil's service, a full Requiem Mass as Phil would have loved, and it was beautiful. The Samoan choir from our parish led the singing. The Croatian choir sang at the end of the service, and the Maori group was singing as Phil was being carried out of the church, once again, on the shoulders of the pallbearers.

If using a word like magnificent is appropriate then this is how I would describe Phil's funeral. I have no doubt that a part of me had removed myself from the depth of my grief so that I could be strong and make Phil proud of me. There was an unexplained strength in between my tears.

Walking up to the altar to give the eulogy I felt proud. I asked Phil to be with me as I made my way up the few steps. I held my head up high to share those words that I had written the night before—those words that came so easily from my heart. I remember feeling strong and present during the eulogy and on a number of occasions was told by others that you would have heard a pin drop during those moments when I spoke. I believe that Phil was proud of me as I read what was written the night before:

We are all shocked at Phil's sudden passing which is why I felt I needed to share with you some moments of his life during the past few months.

On November 8, 2004, his forty-eighth birthday, Phil was diagnosed with an extremely aggressive small cell carcinoma cancer. He insisted that we still go on our Caribbean cruise a few days later, and it was the best thing we did. Not only was it the most wonderful holiday together, but it allowed Phil to really think about what he was facing and to get to a place within himself where he felt that the decisions made would be his and his alone.

The reason he kept his condition from so many people was because firstly he did not want to worry you and secondly he did not want to be treated any differently by his colleagues or to see any sadness in your eyes.

Up until approximately four weeks before his passing, Phil's only noticeable symptom was the lymphoedema in his left arm which he explained to those who did not know his circumstances as being a gym injury. We lived our lives as normally as we could, not as Phil being someone suffering from cancer .but of someone truly "living" with cancer.

From the time of his diagnosis until Tuesday of last week we spent only two nights in a hospice to get his pain relief sorted. The rest of the time he was at home and in fact on Tuesday he did not even want to see a night through at Auckland Hospital. I believe that Philip chose not to make it through the night on Tuesday. He had said what he needed to say to his immediate family members. He felt assured that I was being taken care of. Then from 8.30 P.M. until he passed at 11.11 P.M., we shared the perfect time together. He was lucid, and we were able to communicate until the last forty five minutes or so. His passing was perfect. That night he referred to Jesus as *his mate,* and I believe deeply in my heart that he is now with his mate.

The reason that I am telling you this is so that you all know that Phil was actually spared of great suffering, and, whilst we all prayed for a miracle, I believe our prayers were answered and Philip did receive a miracle.

The decisions that Phil made for himself during these past months were perfect.

I have never witnessed such courage and bravery as I did in Philip during those months, and I don't believe that I will ever see it again.

I know that it is natural to feel cheated and angry, and Phil would understand your need to feel that way. I believe he would not want you to stay that way for too long, and if you are struggling then ask him to assist you through those feelings. He will answer your prayers and give you strength.

Phil's time with us was too short. However let us learn from this remarkable man. His capacity to love was like nothing I had ever seen before and nothing gave him more joy than to know he had helped someone in some way. He continuously gave of himself and was always the peacemaker.

Let us remember him for what he did best...to Love... He wanted everybody to be united in love, to be reconciled with one another, and most importantly he wanted to assist people on how to love themselves.

He showed me how to love to a depth that I did not think was humanly possible. He showed me how to receive love and to understand that I was worthy of his love.

Whilst we all held onto the belief and hope for a different outcome right up until that last day, what got us through these past five months was the knowledge that this path had been perfectly placed to assist us with this final stage of Phil's earthly life.

Thank you all for showing Phil just how loved and how loveable this great man was. You gave him a tremendous gift during these past weeks.

Whilst my heart will never fully recover from this event, Phil gave me the greatest gift in his final hours. He told me that he would now be *my* angel. He said that he would always take care of me and that when I looked up to the stars that he would be there.

This gift is what will help me to go on with my life without your physical presence my love.

An emotional memory was the gathering of a group of my parents' Croatian friends at the front of the church who sang a beautiful Croatian hymn. This brought many a tear to their fellow country people. Phil so loved the Croatian culture and did his best to learn many words. However the poor chap was often the cause of much laughter as he attempted to put a sentence together, often not making much sense at all or at times totally confusing everyone around him.

My most painful memory of the hearse leaving the church grounds was of my father leaning over with one arm on Phil's casket sobbing as his fourth son, "Philipi," was to be taken away. I moved towards my dad and put my arms around him as I still felt strong.

Phil so loved my dad and would often refer to him as a cameo act, particularly the way he laughed and told stories in his strong Croatian accent.

Dad is a performer and a loud one at that. In telling a story, or imitating someone, he would be standing up, waving his arms around and laughing with that very large round smile of his. Phil would then holler with his huge laugh and be clapping his hands two or three times at a very slow beat to acknowledge his approval of dad's, often crazy story.

Phil loved the loudness that came with our family. Whilst for us children it was typical and we would not even think of the intensity of conversation or the level at which it was spoken, for Phil this was very new. He soon embraced the passion, as he often referred to it, that came with our culture.

Thankfully we have a lot of family video available, and on it is Phil—or somewhere in the back ground is Phil's laugh. We had many a family gathering with the nieces and nephews wandering around with the video camera taking shots of us all and of course things that they should not have been taking shots of!

One favourite scene that comes to mind is when Phil was cutting up the turkey during one of my father's birthday parties, and somehow this turkey ended up on the kitchen floor. We all laughed as my brother Nick said to Phil rather loudly and full of humour, "That piece is your's Phil," to which Phil responded with his equally infectious laugh!

Phil's wake was at the Dalmatian club and it was a feast, just as he would have wanted it. There were many stories and speeches, many tears and a beautiful serenade by the Dalmatian people. It was a celebration of a beautiful man who loved people, loved his food and who would have been there somewhere watching and feeling joyous.

Phil loved our cultural food and was also affectionately known in our family as "two stroke" because of the slow speed at which he ate, not like the rest of us in the family. Mom ate at a very high speed just in case of course we might possibly go without! We would often be gazing at the table laden with dessert as we salivated and waited whilst Phil slowly finished off his first course, albeit his second or third helping!

Lance was Phil's boxing pal and he got up at the wake to tell a story which had us all laughing out loud. Lance would often give Phil a lot of stick about his boxing and would get him on the ground and give him a bit of a pummeling every now and then. On the night that Phil passed away Lance came home from a family celebration. Not knowing of Phil's passing, he ended up having a little play fight with his son Jake, who hit him in the process and resulted in Lance having a serious black eye! Lance described this occurrence in his usual humorous manner and how he felt certain the black eye that he received that night from such a soft hit was actually from Phil and a well deserved one at that!

We all thoroughly enjoyed the story. I recall sitting across from my brother Antony as he sat there with his eleven broken ribs from the accident he had two weeks earlier and was having to hold himself with every quiet laugh he managed to squeeze out.

At the end of this long day I came home with Zel and Delwyn back to Jervois Road still not fully comprehending what had happened. The day was huge, and I don't believe that I engaged at all in my own feelings. You are surrounded by people who are trying to comfort you. However often it is you trying to comfort others. I was trying to stay alert through it all. What I remember about the end of the day is the absolute exhaustion which had begun to roll in like a very slow fog.

When I first came home from the hospital after Phil's death and brought home his bag of belongings I constantly held onto the clothing that he wore, his black shorts and T-shirt. I could still smell him, albeit the distinct smell of the cancer, but at least I could smell him. Logically I knew that this was not a healthy thing to do but just for those few days it was something that I needed to do.

Things changed however upon coming home from the funeral. There was this obsessive urgency that arose in me that had to be rid of everything which reminded me of the cancer. Zel and Delwyn came through the house with me with a large rubbish bag as I began room by room to throw away anything that remotely reminded me of the disease. All medications, vitamins, potions, special drinks, doctors' documents all had to go. I even had to dispose of the same shorts and T-shirt which only days earlier I could not part with. It was vital for me that somehow I erase the smell of the cancer and the horror that this disease had left in my memory.

That night Catherine slept in the bed with me. During the night I awoke to my immediate thought of "Oh my God, Phil if only you were in the lounge room next door." Almost immediately in my heart I heard, "But

I am only in the room next door." It was a very clear statement. From where it came I don't know, but what I do know was that I felt it.

Unable to sleep, I got up and walked through the house. It felt empty and cold. It was no longer a home. It was bricks and mortar, nothing more. Phil was gone; of that I was certain. As I walked through the hallway in the darkness and as I felt the emptiness of the walls surrounding me, once again I heard in my heart, "It is time for you to leave this house." I responded, "OK honey, but you show me where to go." I then returned to my bed and slept some more.

Only a few hours later Catherine and I were awoken at six o'clock by the sound of my television in the bedroom turning on. There were no cats in the room, no remote controls close by; it just came on, something that had never happened before. We were both startled as I fumbled around trying to find out how it happened but then both felt at peace thinking that somehow Phil was around.

April 16 nine years ago was a very significant time for me as it was the day that Phil proposed marriage to me. Thank God that we do not see our future. How terrible it would have been to know that we would not get the opportunity to renew our vows at our ten year anniversary as we had planned. Here I was on this April 16, and I had just buried my very young husband.

Catherine and I did not get back to sleep after our six o'clock wake up by the television. Once again I needed to cleanse my home of the memories of the previous days. The lounge was now empty. There was no casket, and his cream lazy boy chair was also empty. The room was covered along all walls with flowers which gave off the most beautiful aroma. This smell was suffocating for me. I could not tolerate it. It kept taking me back to the days when Phil lay here—days which on a conscious level I could not cope with and disassociated myself from.

Now this aroma was trying to take me back there, back to the reality of what had occurred, and it was still somewhere I did not want to go. "At least then he was here" I thought.

Catherine assisted me in taking most of the flowers up to my Parish that morning and other bouquets I distributed to friends and family. Still, I was not ready to feel the extent of my loss.

That day our entire family gathered at Zel's home for a lovely family lunch. It was upon driving to their home in Parnell that I knew in my heart to return to live in Parnell, the area where I lived when Phil and I first met and where we were eventually married.

The following day I phoned my friend Dawn who was a real estate agent and who had been assisting me prior to Phil's death to look for a suitable home which never appeared. Suddenly I knew exactly what I wanted. I described it to her, and two days later I had signed a deal on the perfect place for me. In fact, it so happened that there was already an offer on this particular home which just so happened to fall through an hour before I placed my offer, so the timing was perfect.

This was another example of the continued synchronicity which began to occur since Phil's death that led me to truly believe my life was being directed. All I needed to do was to trust, especially to trust my own intuition.

Yes my angel Phil was keeping to his word and directing me. This was what I deeply felt.

TEN

Coming Out
of the Haze

The next twelve days were unbelievably busy. I sorted through my possessions, had a garage sale and prepared to leave a home that I was once so attached to and could not have conceived of leaving. Now not only was I leaving it but also without Phil, on my way to commence a life on my own, and I could not wait to get away from it.

During my packing there were many tasks I could not do, such as handling Phil's clothing. I was not ready to part with any of them so others graciously moved them to my new home for me. Whilst delivering items to my new home often it felt as though Phil was already there, and others sensed the same thing. Jervois Road for me was now just as weather that had turned cold and dark.

The smallest bedroom in my new home was to be Phil's room and was where his belongings were tidily placed. The first time I entered this room I knelt at the wardrobe where his clothing now hung and slowly moved through each item, bringing various garments to my face. I was desperately trying to recapture Phil as he was before his diagnosis, his scent, remembering the times when he wore certain articles of clothing, remembering his healthy body, just remembering him. Whilst this ritual was agony for me I continued to do it for many months after his death. It seemed worth the pain just trying to remember Phil as he once was, to breathe in what I could whilst his scent was still there.

My own journaling had not occurred at all since early March. I could not sit still long enough to be silent with my feelings. I had to stay on the move. Accessing my pain this way during those final weeks was something I knew not to do, not yet anyway.

On the evening of Friday April 22, ten days after Phil's death, I was alone in the evening and did not feel the need to have anyone stay overnight with me. Alone I hopped into our very large bed, with Fergus also snuggled on the duvet by my feet. Apart from the soft light that came from my bedside lamp, the rest of this large room was in darkness.

As I turned towards my bedside cabinet to my left, I picked up my pen and journal knowing that my time had come. I felt ready to begin the next stage of my journey, to access what was so deeply lodged inside me and what I knew had to be released.

There was a hesitation for me. I was aware that once this process commenced, I would have to continue with it. It was uncharted territory, so I did not know what feelings would erupt or for how long this pain would last. All I knew to do was to start, to let my hand and feelings flow, and this was how my story started as I sat up alone in what was once our bed.

My darling Phil has gone—departed from this earth to be with God, his friend Kevin and his mom and dad. The past six weeks have been a nightmare. I arrived home on a Tuesday, and four Tuesdays later he was gone. It aches to write. The memory of the twelve hours before and after his death are such a nightmare for me. They keep replaying in my head and will not leave me. I did not want Phil to leave this earth in a state of non acceptance of his impending death. I pray that he was at peace; I feel that he was. My greatest heartache tonight as I write is to hope and pray that he did not feel fear during his final hours. He was so hopeless and helpless. This big man who loved life so much could not move his body. He had surrendered. It aches for me to write about it.

There were only eight days in which to move from my house which made each day incredibly busy. At times I felt like I was a machine, without a moment to stop. I was incredibly resilient and even returned to the gym during this time, as if I did not have enough to do. I had to fill each moment. Sitting still was not an option, so I just got on with what had to be done until I moved.

Seven days after Phil's funeral, I attended our regular Saturday evening mass. Sitting in our usual seat without him was heart wrenching for me. It was also very difficult for the rest of the congregation to see me there alone.

Doing everything for the first time without him was difficult, as was driving home alone in the dark, through the same streets, past the same shop window, getting out of the car and walking into an empty house. The cats were all still there to greet me which comforted me. All three mysteriously appeared from nowhere in the dark and waiting patiently for me to unlock the door—all trying to be the first one in.

Sunday April 24, 2005,

I am now in bed and what I want is to shrivel up and die, to get thinner and thinner and leave this place. However I know that Phil would not want that for me. Why did you leave me Honey? How will I live my life without you?

Such a busy day today, I awoke at 4.30 A.M. and have this need to get up straight away, to get into my day as soon as I can and be busy so that I don't feel the pain so intensely.

Monday April 25 was a public holiday, so friends were assisting me in clearing and getting things ready for my move. It was a very difficult day for me. I gave away my thirteen year old cat Rudi to my friend Celia. Rudi was the cat I owned before Phil and I met, and as attached as I was to him I knew not to take all three cats with me to my new home.

Rudi was waiting in my bedroom with the door closed, and once Celia arrived we both sat on my bed with Rudi on her lap actually enjoying being stroked by his new mom. Here I was saying goodbye to yet something else in my life that gave me so much joy.

I wept and wept as this beautiful woman with her soft Samoan accent gave me a kind telling off as I shared with her that I did not want to live any more and that there was no point now without Phil. "Don't be so selfish," Celia said to me. Yes, I agree with her as to how much more hurt I would create in even contemplating the thought of ending my own life when I had just witnessed Phil fight for his until his final breaths.

Another reason for my darkness that morning resulted from my investigation on the internet about what small cell carcinoma cancer really meant. I needed to sit and read about it. Prior to Phil's death, I really did not want to know and believed that his outcome would be different.

That morning I was like a woman obsessed, reading statistics, causes, symptoms, everything I could find. It was important that I face those three words that would once awaken me during the night—the words I was terrified of. I had decided that morning I would no longer give them such power over me, to paralyze me as they once had.

Sitting in the dark at my computer with only the light of the screen lighting up the room, I was able to face the horror that I ran from for those months—to truly see the harsh reality that at the advanced stage of Phil's cancer he had no chance for survival. No matter what amount of chemotherapy, natural products or positive thoughts we put forward, Phil could not have survived.

I felt rather stoic upon reading all of this. I got up from my computer desk and walked away as if I had conquered my fear, but, later on the following day when my friend Lois came over, these three words took me down again one last time. Lois walked into my dining room and held me tightly as I was crying out loud, "He did not have a chance." And Lois, being beautiful Lois, placed her hands around my face, looked into my flooded eyes, and, with her own tears slowly building, replied, "No love, he did not."

Tuesday April 26, 2005,

Today was my worst day since the funeral, and my folks came over to calm me down. By the end of the night I could not function. Alone I lay on the couch for the night, wrapped up in a blanket. My world was black, and I saw nothing ahead for me.

Tuesdays were awful for me now, and this one ended much the same as my stress levels hit an all time high. I had misplaced the keys to my car. At home many of my friends turned everything upside down throughout my home and the surrounding boxes for hours to search for them. In the end they turned out to be at the delicatessen across the road. Often it is not the big things that cause the breakdown but the little things that can tip you over the edge. That day, the amount of distress that the simple loss of my keys had caused was totally disproportionate to the reality of what was really happening in my life and what was yet to come.

A few days later I needed to collect a courier package waiting for me in Parnell, and, unbeknown to me as I drove in the driveway, I realized that the courier company was next to the home which I rented ten years earlier when I first met Phil. Upon collecting the package I drove to a position and parked my car in the driveway where I could sit and look at this little townhouse, recalling some of the memories of that December in 1994 when I first met Phil and we began dating.

I sat in my car outside my old home, the rain was not heavy just a constant drizzle, so much so that I had to turn my windscreen wipers on occasionally as my vision of the house was becoming blurred. I felt very alone as my tears began. My sadness was indescribable as I thought of Phil and wondered if he was happy now. At that moment I saw a huge rainbow form. It totally covered this little townhouse from side to side as if it was an archway leading into the house. At that moment I really felt Phil's presence. I cried and cried as he felt so close to me yet I could not touch him; I could not reach out; I could not cuddle him. I wanted to share this event with someone. Who could I call? At that precise moment I received a text from my friend Danielle.

Today the girls and I were talking about Phil. I haven't felt his presence since last week, and the girls were asking if he was happy. In the next instant a big bright, colorful and full rainbow appeared to the right. Unbelievable, it was a wonderful and warming experience. He is with us! I want to tell the world. I hope that your day has been kind.

Immediately I telephoned Danielle to also share my experience. I felt such joy to somehow know that Phil was giving me a sign that he was happy. Was I clutching at anything or was this really a sign? On that day I chose to believe that it was a sign. I needed to believe it was a sign.

Danielle made a beautiful quilt for Phil with the intention of giving it to him. He did not get to see it, so this quilt was taken to his wake and signed by the many who attended.

On the same day as this rainbow occurrence Zel and I were having a beautiful conversation. He was feeling rather low, and it was my time to be strong for him, so I suggested that he pray to Phil for strength that day. Zel found this difficult to do, so he asked me to, to which I replied "No Zel, all you need to do is say, Philip, Remember Me." After a brief silence Zel quietly said to me "Those were the exact words that I wrote on Phil's quilt at the wake." This for me was yet another moment where I felt Phil's presence and that he was at work in healing our broken hearts.

During my final two days at Jervois Road I sold many items of furniture and possessions that I would not be taking to my new home. Others assisted in doing this for me on the Saturday morning whilst I remained busy inside so that I did not have to see the items disappear into the hands of others. I would whisk in and out bringing food, making tea, working in the house, but I could not be present whilst these articles left and once again my defense mechanisms had kicked in which was fine by me.

Attending Mass that evening I thought would be easier, since it was no longer the first time. I had conquered that one the week before, or so I thought. As I sat alone in the church in our usual pew, I looked up at the mosaic that covered most of the altar. In front of it was the most beautiful cross with Jesus on it.

I had finally stopped that day. My body was still and my mind was also still as I looked up at the cross. Slowly I was becoming aware of the moment, my tiredness and how my body felt. For the first time in a long time I was in the present moment, and slowly I could feel the grief beginning to build like the wave of a tsunami. I could feel it emerging from my stomach and moving up into my chest as if I was standing on the shore and feeling the rumbling beneath my feet as it came closer to me, yet I could not move. I just had to watch, to feel what was building within me.

Unable to stop the tears that slowly began to build I raised myself from my seat, took a couple of steps across the aisle, stopped as I looked up at the cross again and moved towards the left of the church. I moved through the pews with my body facing forward so that the people behind me could not see my face. I proceeded towards the bathroom as quietly as I could and once there I allowed the emotion to release from within me.

What I did not realize would happen was the extent of pain that would be released at that moment when I allowed myself to be still for those initial moments. The quiet tears now became uncontrollable, so much so that I was unable to stop or draw a breath calmly. All of a sudden my grief arrived—the reality of all my loss—of Phil, my cat Rudi, my home that we shared, our belongings, my dream, my security. My life, as I knew it was over, and it would never be the same.

An indescribable darkness enveloped me as my tears became longer and louder. I was well aware of the echoing of my crying in the corridor and the depth from which it was emerging from me, but I had no control once it began to be released. On some level it did not matter, just as during the early hours of April 13 on the quiet Auckland streets outside the hospital and nothing could hold it back.

Monsignor Cronin came to retrieve me from the bathroom and held me up. I said to him that I could not go on—that it was not worth going on without Phil, so he took me up to the Presbytery where I remained for the duration of the Mass. Whilst I was reassured by him I could get through this, my thoughts were that I did not want to, nor did I believe that it was possible.

Tonight is unbearable. I cannot believe that he is gone. My heart bleeds for him. There is no point in being here anymore. What is the point? Catherine is coming to stay with me. I cannot be alone tonight.

ELEVEN

My Painful Reality

Monday May 2, 2005,

Here I am lying on the floor in my empty office gazing at a photo of Phil whilst the removal men are taking the larger items from what once used to be my home. The weather has now turned. It is a grey autumn day and it feels somber just as I do today, as I get ready to leave my life as I knew it behind.

Last night Catherine and I went over to my new home. It was the first time she saw it, and, like me when she got to the top level, she shouted, "I love it"! We were both so happy and excited. In fact, everything that is happening for me all feels so right.

During our deep sharing together it became clear to us both that I write a book—the book Phil so wanted to write about his journey. I then felt even more excitement about my future. I forgot about my reality for that moment as I projected into what I saw would be a happy life for me.

It was not until we went into Phil's room later in the evening that my sadness and tears returned. As we went through his clothing that was carefully placed in the wardrobe, once again I could smell him.

Later that afternoon…

Here I am in my new home, and it feels nice and fresh. I am so happy to be here. The move has been both exciting and stressful and there is such a big job ahead of me to put everything away. However I do not care. All that matters is that I am away from Jervois Road and in my new surroundings. The rest will happen in due course.

I have brought only two cats with me. Chi has been going ape around the house, meowing and then did a big puke. Fergus took a good look around the entire house for about two hours, had a good sniff everywhere, then found a sunny spot and thought, yeah, this will do and settled down to sleep for the rest of the afternoon!

By leaving Jervois Road I was able to escape some of my darkness, particularly the memories of the cancer during those final weeks. I also wanted to run from my happy memories, to block out the physical things that reminded me of the extent my loss. Some people thought that I moved too soon, but I followed my heart, and, once I stepped foot into my new home, I had no doubt that the decision I made was the right one.

My home soon became a very special place for me. It was on a main road, something we did not like about Jervois Road. It was well enclosed which kept away the noise, and it was very private. Being in a complex, I felt secure. There were neighbors close by, and never did I feel frightened during the night being on my own, which now was how life was for me.

Being in a different environment was refreshing. Whilst I am not one for clichés, it felt like a new beginning, especially by letting go of things from my old home so that I could create a new surrounding for myself. It was important for me to be in the right frame of mind and think positively about my future when I put my home together so that it reflected me, who I was and who I was becoming. I took my time over the next few months to do this task instead of rushing in when I was not yet ready.

Today I awoke excited at the thought of getting on with my day.

There has actually been a mix of some excitement about feeling slightly better but guilt for having this joy in my new surroundings. Now that the evening has arrived my sadness at not having Phil is here, and my heart is aching. I miss him so much, yet I know that I must sit quietly and grieve Phil and not try to run from this pain.

Today I decided to let go of Chi to Phil's brother Paul. It is too painful for me to have Chi here as it is too much of a reminder of Phil. I feel that soon he too will die, and I cannot watch him die also. I feel selfish and cruel, but I just cannot keep him here.

Chi was unsettled with the move, and as I thought he died within six months of Phil. I was grateful not to have to witness this. On some level I let go of two of our cats without any feeling attached. I closed myself down to any more loss at that time.

On this day I went to the supermarket to get my groceries as a single person for the first time in ten years. It was a terrible experience having to shop only for myself and completely alter my choices about what to buy.

It was manageable until I arrived at the checkout. The operator realized who I was and said to me about Phil, "Oh, he is the one who just died." This took my breath away as I had not yet used the *d* word. How I described what had happened to Phil was that he had passed away. Death seemed too final for me at this early stage. On some level I was still having difficulty with the notion that Phil had gone forever.

I do not recall anything until my next memory of being in the car park and beginning to softly weep with my head low as I reached over to remove my grocery bags from the trolley. Still facing the ground there was a presence to my right. It felt like a whisk of air coming past me. As I looked up through my swollen eyes, there was my dear friend and therapist David Chaloner standing there with a gentle smile. This for me was an unbelievable feeling. One minute I felt nothing; the next it felt like I was experiencing an angel at my side at the perfect time and the perfect place.

When I realized through my tears that it was David, I said to him "He is not coming home is he?"

David softly replied, "No, he is not."

Once David had described to me the synchronicity of how he just so happened to be there at that moment, it confirmed to me yet again that I was now being carried through my part of this journey. As difficult as this would be at times, my angel Phil would ensure that I made it through. Whilst I had a knowing that my work and learning was to commence once Phil had passed away, on that day I realized it had already begun and at a more rapid pace than I had anticipated. My lesson in truly trusting about the remainder of my life was before me.

My trust was to be tested within days. Once again I had the finality of my life with Phil thrown in front of me when the death certificate arrived.

> Today started off good for me. I had my hair done which really lifted me. Then I came home to Phil's death certificate in the mail, and I saw that *d* word again. Oh my God it has happened; Philip died, and he is not coming home. My day felt sad from then on and got worse as evening fell, so much that Delwyn came and stayed the night. The grief has arrived.
>
> New Zealand **Death Certificate.** Philip Joseph Morrow. 12 April 2005. Metastatic Small Cell Carcinoma of Unknown Primary 6 months.

How dare they all throw this in my face. I was angry that I was constantly having it brought home to me that Philip died. There it was in black and white. The horror and reality of Phil's death had finally hit me—the harsh fact that he would not be returning, and I would never see him again.

I began to wear his wedding band, a ring which he referred to as his mirror since it was so big—one he said that made a statement. I also wore the cross that he once wore around his neck. I just needed to clutch onto the physical of Phil in some way.

Saturday May 7,

I have just returned from the movies with Delwyn, Dominique and a few other girls. It was my first time going out at night without Phil. Thankfully they picked me up. I would not have coped with driving on my own. I enjoyed going out, however I did not want to go to dinner afterwards. I just needed to come home and be alone.

Returning home and turning on the TV, I heard an interview with Lauren Bacall within minutes. She described her journey with Humphrey Bogart during his illness. She said, *The person who is ill sets the tone; you must respect what they want.* She continued saying that they never lived as if he was dying, and they never talked about it.

This was for me to hear and has really helped in my questions on whether I should have done anything differently with Phil since we did not speak openly about his death. Whilst I now feel quite empty that this exchange did not occur for me, as it was something I needed, it was what Phil wanted, and that was the most important thing.

Today I have the lonely pain for Phil. Most of the time it is just a hideous, continuous, dull ache. Then I have moments where it just hits me like a bolt of lightning, and the pain can be so unbearable. Is this how I will feel for the rest of my life?

My dreams at this time were vivid and so real. It was as if Phil was present in the room when I would awaken from them. At times I did wonder how much of this was imagination. Was I searching for a sign or was he in fact present in some other form, hovering to assist me through these dark times and letting me know that he was near?

Tuesday May 10 at 5.10 A.M.,

I dreamt about Phil last night. It was so real. I could see him at a distance in the store. I text him, *spunky chick in shop* and then spotted him coming towards me through the fruit and vegetable department. Here was this large man towering over all of the other customers, having a chat with the ladies in the deli before he came to greet me with his usual kiss. I awoke. It felt as though he was there, but he was not, and then I remembered he would not be coming back.

It was now a month since Phil's funeral and life continued. The world did not stop and it was time to go back to the normal routine in our lives although I no longer had one. My life with Phil worked very well with a good balance of work, recreation, socializing and time for myself. Now however, I had no idea of what normal meant for me. I had to redefine it and rediscover a routine that worked well for me.

Cooking my meals was no longer a major task. Keeping the house clean was now a breeze. How on earth would I work out my day of what to do, when and with whom?

There was still a steady stream of visitors and this I loved, however I soon discovered I could not keep this up. Everyone wanted to talk about Phil, about me and how I was doing. I would attempt to remain strong and stoic for others, although it became apparent that I was putting a lid on my own process and that the constant talking was beginning to drain me. Soon I became rather anxious every time the phone would ring wondering how I could possibly accommodate another visitor. It became a double edged sword as I needed both the support and the space. It was therefore time to re-visit my own personal boundaries and learn how to say no to people for the simple reason that I needed to place my own self care first and foremost. The tiredness was beginning to hit me, and as much as I was aware of this I was still not sure how to stop and rest.

One of the most difficult journeys in my life began when I was fourteen. I was getting dressed to go to my first disco ever. I was In my jeans, a long white sleeved shirt and a denim waist coat (which by the way was fashionable at the time). For a moment I remember thinking how nice I looked.

In an instant my thinking changed and the thought went through my mind that I looked fat. I continued to observe myself, turning from side to side, and around so that my bum was facing the mirror. As I turned my head right around to get a view of my rear, once again I told myself that I was fat.

The reality was that I was actually rather lean, certainly within normal proportions with my very tall build and Croatian heritage. Unfortunately my vulnerable young mind could not absorb this fact. What became ingrained in my belief system in that moment was that I was fat, unattractive and not very feminine at all. This deadly seed led to many years of struggling for self acceptance and perfection in order to be loveable and acceptable in this world of mine.

My belief was that in order to be feminine and lovable, I had to be slim. Therefore at a young age I learned how to lose weight and keep my body at a prepubescent state so much that I did not menstruate for three years. At that early age I also discovered that food could dull pain. Comfort eating stopped me feeling and facing what was really happening in my life. There were the typical teenage struggles in becoming a woman, and, later in my adult struggles as I longed for the freedom to be myself, I still had no idea of who I actually was.

Whilst I was never one to eat burgers or fried foods or alcohol or ever be tempted by drugs or smoking, I learned very soon that what dulled my pain were the sweet foods. It did not need to be a lot, but, enough to alter my thinking and often put me to sleep.

Over the years, with an enormous amount of work and support, healing in this area of my life has gradually occurred, and I was able to slowly recover from this self imposed prison of obsession and rules. My recovery was very slow and certainly never perfect, with many a relapse as I always searched for some sweetness in my life during times of stress.

My greatest battle to overcome was my need for perfection in so many areas of my life—my studies, work and career, earning ability, capabilities in the home and of course the external appearances that I felt I had to keep. The distorted thinking often meant seeing a body far larger than it actually was which is an extremely common issue with men and women as we attempt to meet the unrealistic expectations around body size in our society today.

During the last months of Phil's life my body shrunk in size and not intentionally. I was still eating well, but my adrenalin was constantly pumping, and I was burning up so much emotional and physical energy. I would often reach for whatever would give me that instant fix to keep going, and it was often sweet food.

Now here I was living on my own, not having to cook at all in fact. It took me some time before I began to create a decent meal for myself. One of the greatest danger times for me to crave sweet foods was when I was tired. I would reach for anything to keep me going, and temporarily it worked.

Once again I began to relapse into my distorted thinking and have recurrences of using sugar to either keep me awake during the day or to dull my pain. Soon, these recurrences would become more frequent. I would not be eating decent meals, and the mix began to cause me considerable anguish.

My journey of recovery of this difficulty in my life will not be covered in this book. It is documented only for the purpose of demonstrating how grief can manifest itself and once again resurrect old demons that you may have believed were finally laid to rest.

Sunday May 15 at 8.30 P.M.,

I'm not feeling too good. I am high on sugar and am bound to come down with a bang. What sparked this eating of bad food? Perhaps it was my inability to cope with all of these people coming over this afternoon and that Phil would not be with me to hide behind. Fergus is on the bed with me. He is being so attentive. He must be sensing my pain.

For over two months now I have not been eating good meals but instead, too much sugar to keep me going. I have not been taking care of myself at all really.

Honey my pain is so great when I pray to you, and when I talk to you. It is all so much easier when I remain busy. It is when I stop that my heart aches. It aches because I feel your presence and this is yet another reminder that your physical presence is not with me.

I am coping by being strong and stoic and funny, perhaps masking my pain and grief in front of others. It feels time for me to slow down and sit and just be and feel the pain.

Thursday May 19 at 8 p.m.,

Today I have not cried once. I have felt accepting and at peace and rather strong. I've gone from no longer fearing quiet times to now welcoming them. I have gone from not wanting to stop, pray and be silent, to being unable to wait to be in Phil's little room for some quiet time. The funeral director came over and brought Phil's ashes home. They came in two separate boxes, quite heavy actually, quite surreal to think that he is in there.

Phil's room was the smallest spare room in my new home and was where I created a shrine for him. All of his clothing hung in the wardrobe, and the large cream lazy boy chair that he spent his final three weeks in, was positioned in the corner. There was a large dresser which stood about five feet high on which I placed Phil's ashes, our statue of Mary and also Phil's favorite picture of Jesus that rested at the end of his hospital bed the night he died. Other items placed were Phil's private memorabilia such as his work name badges, favourite pens and various trinkets. On top of the box which held his remains, I placed a favourite picture of him which was taken on my 40th birthday, the year before.

In another corner of this room I placed more photos of Phil along with others close to him who had also died: his mom, dad and of course his friend Kevin. More significant belongings were placed on the floor, such as his gym bag still with all of its contents which I had not yet been able to remove.

To the right of the cream lazy boy chair, which I now sat in regularly, were a collection of many books that Phil had read right up until the end, my own daily reading books and journals which I now spent many hours writing in.

It was during the early hours of the morning when the rest of the city would be asleep that I would feel my greatest peace. As soon as I would awaken, no matter how tired I felt, sleeping again would not be an option. Instead I would go into Phil's room and grasp at the joy which was always there for me. Soon this little room became a sanctuary for me where so much of my processing would occur—where I would write thousands of words in my journals, where I would sit and weep as I looked at Phil's photo trying to comprehend what had happened in my life, to us.

As winter was now approaching, I would cover my legs with a blanket, and of course there would never be a show without my buddy Fergus on my lap. This would make writing difficult, but I never had the heart to throw him off my legs. So if it meant placing my journal to his right on the armrest or even on his back as I wrote, so be it. He was happy and was present during the forming of the majority of my journey through these journals.

Often in the early days when I created this little shrine, Fergus would nestle himself into Phil's gym bag, smell, dig and sleep in the bag, or he would go into the wardrobe and rummage through his clothing, smell and meow looking for his dad.

Saturday May 21 at 3.25 P.M.,

I am lying on my bed with Fergus. I miss Phil. I even feel lonely. Prayer does help, living one day at a time helps, but it all still stinks. Today I was in a place of being alone in this world, being single, not a place I ever thought that I would be again, not at forty one anyway. There was such a security for me in knowing that we were together for life, safety from the world. Perhaps a reminder to search for this safety and security in *me*.

Monday May 23,

Today has been a terrible unmanageable day. P.M.T. does not help with matters.

I continue to question if I had done the right thing by not talking about death and dying with Phil. Today in my session with David he reassured me that I did exactly what Phil wanted and that was to let him live in hope, not with the dread of dying around him. David reminded me that this was exactly what Phil wanted.

Once upon a time the thought of living on without Phil was unbearable for me, and life did not seem worth living. Now that some weeks have passed I know that, one day at a time, I can cope and no longer want to die. I think I will hang about for a while longer.

Thursday May 26,

Last night I went out to dinner with some couples. That felt awkward, hence I awoke with the thought of what I have lost, and I ask myself, will I ever have that again in my life? It feels as though nothing or no one will compare.

Before Phil passed away someone said to me that perhaps his death would be for the good of all mankind. I pondered on this and kept that in my thoughts but could not quite get my head around it. This thought has made me cry, yes tears for me. It may be good for man-kind but not that good for me. Perhaps I am being selfish in thinking this way. How is Phil's passing for the good of all mankind? Has his life changed people whom he has known? Has his death changed people's attitudes about their own lives? Will it be people changing their lives through Phil's book? Is this how I should view this, or am I now becoming a victim in my thinking? I hope that I don't. Actually, I will not.

Friday May 27,

Today has been a day of moving forward and free of excruciating pain. Last night I cried myself to sleep, and the pain was unbearable. This morning however I woke up feeling better. That is what I must do. When the pain is there, just feel it, indulge in it, experience it and soon, it will pass.

This week for me has been about letting go of guilt—the guilt that I feel for being alive and Phil not. The guilt I feel for now being able to enjoy my home with only Fergus and not the stress of the other two cats, for the joy of being able to see how important it is to live each day and to realize that this life is only for such a short time.

This I believe is survivor's guilt and is all very normal. Sometimes I reverse the process and contemplate if it was me who died and Phil left behind. What would I want for him? This assists me to rationalize and softens this guilt that I am carrying.

Birthdays were always a celebration for Phil and me. Being a widow at forty one was not something I wanted to acknowledge this year. Sleeping through the day seemed a far easier option. Delwyn kindly brought our entire family together to celebrate my birthday, and we had a lovely evening together.

Last year was very different. I was extremely excited about turning forty, knowing that it would be a turning point in my life. There was a great deal of acceptance around the fact that we had not conceived our own children, and I had already begun to find meaning and purpose in my life without the title of *mother*. You adapt to the notion that your family is the two of you, and we were very excited about our future and the plans we had made together.

Little did I know I had not even scratched the surface of discovering *who* Tanya was and that my most life transforming event was yet to occur.

Saturday June 4,

Today has been a good day. Actually I have had four good days in a row. When I have these good days, guilt steps in, and I try to bring the grief back somehow, feeling that I should be grieving. As if I feel I might forget him if I am not grieving. Perhaps it is part of survivor's guilt, and I should really enjoy the breather whilst it is here.

Tuesday June 7,

My grief has been triggered. TV programs, no Phil, everything in fact is purgatory for me. What a difference from my breather a few days ago. I should have enjoyed it whilst it lasted; you never know when you are going to get hammered again. I really feel him nearby at the moment, or am I just imagining this? Well no, I do feel a presence.

It is two days before my 41st birthday. I wish it was my 81st and that I did not need to go through the next forty years without Phil. Today I felt utter disbelief that he is not with me. Tonight I want to recapture our memories to somehow keep him alive and with me.

I keep thinking that this is some sick joke. I go from acceptance to absolute disbelief that this has happened to me. Somehow, I can accept his fate but not mine. Now I know what they mean by it being the hardest for those who are left behind. As my birthday is approaching I feel very teary eyed and am missing Phil.

This time eight weeks ago was the worst day of my life. Tuesdays will never be the same for me. Father help me. Philip help me.

Friday June 10, 9 P.M.,

I missed writing on my birthday. I could not bring myself to do it. Most of the day felt as though I was not even in my body. I went through the motions of everything and totally escaped my pain by rushing around and eating too much sugary food.

The day before my birthday was all so painful, so I ran from the pain. I did that big exercise class even though I was so tired and did not sleep well from the exhaustion that my body felt. I awoke groggy at 7 A.M., had a terrible morning and felt yuck, rushed around and met a girlfriend for coffee. I held it together, and once that was over I could not hold it together any longer, and I fell apart.

It seemed that my entire morning was just insane. I was running from my reality. I pulled over to the side of the road and listened to all of my birthday messages before I went to see David Chaloner. Here I was, in my car on a busy street crying my eyes out. There were about fourteen messages on my phone. I felt loved by all, but I still felt very alone without Phil. If only there was one message from Phil there, that would be all that I wanted to hear. Thankfully I had an hour with David where I could continue to fall apart—no pressures from anyone. He just allowed me to be.

The evening of my birthday was my family gathering at Zel's. Catherine was to stay the night with me, and two other girlfriends also attended, which I thoroughly enjoyed. Dinner was lovely. We all really laughed, and some of us also cried. There was a photo of Phil just to the side of the dinner table, so part of me imagined that he too was there with us, enjoying the beautiful food, as hollow legs always would.

It was when Delwyn brought out the enormous chocolate torte that mom had made as my birthday cake and everyone was singing "happy birthday" to me that I broke down. My tears began to fall as Delwyn placed the cake in front of me and put both hands on my face and lovingly kissed me as if to say "well done Tanya." Almost immediately my brother Nick very loudly says above all the singing, "Was our singing that bad Tanya," which of course interrupted my grief with a good laugh.

Catherine and I arose very early the next morning to probably one of the coldest days that winter, and we went for a brisk walk, sharing deeply our inner feelings along Auckland's waterfront. In fact it felt rather similar to the early walk that the two of us shared only two days after Phil's diagnosis on the tenth of the month the November before, where I shared my thoughts about Phil's possible death. Here we were again, seven months later, on the tenth of the month as we were now living this reality.

Sunday June 12,

Thank goodness my birthday is over, the first of the firsts without Phil. Today has been a good day, probably because I have taken myself off the sugar for a few days, and as a result my emotions feel more stable and my sleep is better. One of the vital things for my healing at this time is to lead a clean life, to love and respect my body as my vessel that I need to feed well.

Tonight I started the Caribbean photo album of our last holiday together. It felt good to look at those photos, it is all part of my healing, recapturing memories, which on some level allows you to let go, whatever that means.

I often reflect on the synchronicity that has continued to occur in my life both before Phil's diagnosis and of course since his death. I followed my instinct to embark on further studies to be a therapist and consequently this ignited my passion surrounding the grieving process and dedication to work with the terminally ill. We had so many friends and acquaintances diagnosed with cancer and of course both of my parents during their own battles with this hideous disease. Never could I have conceived that these experiences were actually preparing me for what was to be my most important role.

It was now two months after Phil's death and somehow everything seemed darker for me. I would often go back to my resources to read about the grieving process and interpret how my own progress was. Was I following the norm? What could I next expect? When would this hideous pain end, if ever? I became a silent observer of Tanya, the young grieving widow, watching and monitoring her own process.

Somehow this did assist me to logically think my way through when the pain became too great. I was relieved to see that this dip was quite normal once you came out of shock and the painful reality finally hits home of the enormity of your loss. It enabled me to feel that I was normal and not going insane, that one day at a time I had to ride this out as there was no easy route out of the pain, only, through it.

During the times when I was feeling low my thinking would often not be rational, and soon I became aware of the cycle or triggers that could lead me on the downward spiral. I learned to ask myself if I was feeling Hungry, Angry, Lonely or Tired, *(halt)*, and often I would be in one of these states. Once I recognized this fact, it meant taking action by attending to what it was that I needed, such as having a nap or eating something, which then enabled me to recognize the feelings that were present. Sometimes I made the decision to evaluate my thinking which would lead to a change in how I felt and if a change was in fact necessary. Sometimes a change was not necessary, and I simply had to sit with my feelings as it was deep sadness which I tried not to run from.

Saturday June 18, 6.15 A.M.,

I have just woken up from a dream that has really upset me as Phil was so real. There was sadness between us. It was about children and the fact that we could not have them. When I awoke for a moment I had forgotten that he was gone. That was bliss, but then I remembered.

Last night whilst watching a funny movie I laughed, but what followed was this flash about never hearing Phil's laugh again which brought on this terrible burst of grief. It does not take much, only the slightest memory can trigger this terrible pain. You have to be ready at all times as you don't really know when your grief will be triggered or what will trigger it. I am not surprised that people annihilate themselves with substances just to escape this pain.

I am still keeping too much sweet foods off my diet which is great. What it does however is bring out my feelings. I am not burying them. The feeling that I am trying to keep away is anger, and today I felt angry at God. I could not imagine why I had to endure this level of pain in my life. I thought enough already!

Tuesday June 21,

I feel nuts and stressed, so much so that I have the shakes. Last night was not a good night. With a lot of tension and adrenalin inside, it felt like an anxiety attack. I began to worry about my life and whether I would be all right in my future. Why does everything feel so insane for me at the moment? If feels as though I have regressed so much.

When I ask myself if I did not have to worry about any of these little things that are present for me, what would be left for me is the loss of Phil. Is the worry about the small stuff one way of taking me out of my real grief—yet another mechanism I use to escape my pain?

It is now the evening, and I have just read about surrendering of self. After all, what other option do I have? Sometimes I feel that I need to totally throw myself into God's hands. How else can I live? How do I do that without being a religious fanatic? I don't think I would ever be that, but I need to get through this, and I know of no other way.

Today during my counseling session with David he enabled me to recognize my burnout. I need to halt, slow down and feel.

This time was clearly tumultuous for me, at times I felt insane as was evident in my journaling. The shock was wearing off and the finality of this occurrence in my life was constantly being thrust into my face by the smallest of memories, and I was not yet ready to accept this level of closure. A laugh, a song or a smell would be all that it would take to trigger me on a downward spiral as I remembered that Phil actually did die and worst of all, that he was never coming home.

Wednesday June 22,

Today I awoke at 4.30 A.M. to a lot of pain in my heart as the disbelief about Phil continues. Last night I chose to comfort eat in an attempt to escape this hideous pain. Nothing can alleviate it; it feels too great to endure right now. I don't know who I am anymore or what my place in the world is or what my reason for being here is. I am not doing my accountancy or counseling, so what am I? What is my future; where am I going? Last night in bed I was trying to reflect on *who* I was, and I needed to anchor myself down to a time in my life when I felt complete, but I could not.

My thoughts were deviating from the pain of my loss of Phil and going to the familiar of thinking about my body size and worrying about my food intake. The reality was that my weight was well within normal range. When one needs to escape pain, those facts do not matter, and my mind was playing tricks on me.

Moving into the cycle of dissatisfaction with myself was one way of removing myself from the feelings of the present moment, which of course was pain. That evening I felt fat, and I had convinced myself that my belly was empty and needed filling with something.

It was in fact my heart that was empty and needed filling that evening. I needed to nurture myself on another level, but I went back to the old habit of comforting myself with some sweet food again.

That cold winter night I went to bed feeling an aloneness and a terrible despair that I had not yet experienced. I did not know where to turn any more. Which direction was my life now going? If this was how painful it was going to remain then I did not want it. That night I did not want to feel any more pain, and the only way I knew how to escape it was to fill the emptiness inside with some comfort food. This is such a common behavior for many—one that I would severely chastise myself for.

I awoke the following morning feeling just as hopeless as I did when I lay my head down the night before. Somehow though it was worse now. I was still alive and, I had to face my day. I went to sleep in the dark, and I awoke in the darkness, both outside my home and inside my being. My world felt black and I could not help but wonder what was the point of being here if this was how my life would be.

I stood in my white toweling robe with my arms cross, leaning on my kitchen bench staring at the digital clock on the oven. It was six-thirty. The thought of facing another day feeling this emptiness and pain seemed like an impossible task. I did not feel present, grounded or that there was any substance to me. In fact I felt robbed of everything that once formed the identity of who I was.

Usually when I was this low I needed to be on my own, but this morning was different. I could not face myself or the day that lay ahead. I phoned my therapist, David, opening up to him of the emptiness that had enveloped me, choking me. What on earth was I now here for?

I wanted David to fill this emptiness as I poured out my anguish. I knew that this was not possible. I was searching for something outside of myself to fill this gap. His words to me were simple yet profound: He shared with me that those whom have had the greatest spiritual experiences in their lives and discovered who they really were, are those who at one point in their lives had lost everything or felt as though they had lost everything, including themselves.

This was what I needed to be reminded of that morning, and immediately I recognized I had hit my rock bottom and there was nowhere further for me to fall. At that present moment I was at my lowest point and experiencing my greatest emptiness which I knew needed to be filled. It was important that my fulfillment came from within and not from short term external things or people. My tank needed to be filled with all of what I knew as the truth, my truth. If I did not go within, then ultimately, I would go without.

After my conversation with David on this June morning I realized that the time in my life when I felt most complete was during Phil's illness, particularly those final four weeks of his life. This was who I was. It was at this time when I accomplished the most meaningful task in my life, and nothing could compare to this for me. Whilst some of those memories of caring for Phil during his final weeks are my most horrific time, I would not exchange them. I was giving unconditionally to another human being, and it was something that came so naturally for me. A thousand men could not have dragged me away from my task at that time.

It then occurred to me that if I did nothing else during my time on this earth, this experience of nursing Phil was enough for me to hold and know that I was worthy simply for "who" I was. It did not matter what I did for a job, how much money I was able to earn, how I looked or what the scales said. I was worthy for what I gave at that time in my life to Phil.

Thursday June 23,

I am worthy and nothing else needs to be said. What I gave to Phil of myself during his final months was my greatest gift to another human being. Nothing else could compare, and I need not accomplish anything else in this life in order to feel my real worth. In fact I feel rather privileged that God chose me for this task and felt I was strong enough and worthy enough to walk next to Phil during his final act.

These are the things I need to hold, to help me in this life which I often find to be such a struggle—a struggle to accept self, to cope with the stresses of the everydayness, to nurture myself. I need to come to a point of knowing and understanding that I enter this world alone and I leave this world alone, with nothing, no possessions, just my soul.

At this moment my core fear of being alone is with me. I stand alone; it is now me and God, no one, or nothing else. This was what I observed about Phil during his final hours. It was he and God in the end, not even me.

TWELVE

Finding Peace

It seemed I just could not comprehend the fact that Phil died and would not be returning home. As much as I attempted to escape at times, the reality would continue to be triggered by many things and the finality of it would tear my heart out.

This was how it could be for the rest of my life. I had to stop myself from thinking this way and attempt to take one day at a time. I had to break my future down into manageable segments. Each morning I would spend time in Phil's room either journaling or simply sitting and coming to terms with yet another day ahead for me.

This daily routine was necessary and kept me grounded at that time. I felt as though I could easily become off centre if I did not take part in my daily ritual. On occasion my routine seemed too rigid, however this was the extent I needed to go to in order to get through each day which otherwise could easily overwhelm me.

My anxiety would arise about the uncertainty of my future. It was the first time in eleven years that I was single in this big world—the world that I so often feared as a child. Now here I was once again facing some of my old demons, and it was now up to me, Tanya, the adult woman, to discover my own path and confidently walk it. I knew that somehow I had to go within to find this confidence. No longer did I have Phil as my solid sounding board. Yes, I could pray and speak to him that way, but it meant sitting still and listening, and what often accompanied my stillness was the pain of my loss.

Tuesday July 5,

I have just completed Phil's memory book. This keeps me connected to him in some way, and, whilst it has been very healing to do, I still feel in a space of not wanting to move on. How can I move on when I don't even know where I am moving on to, or I don't even know what moving on means for me? Do I even know me?

One of the techniques I knew of, to assist in my healing process was to create a memory book of Phil, similar to a scrap book, like I would have kept as a teenager. Whilst I logically knew this was a means of healing, a part of me also used it as a means of keeping his memory alive. I did not want him or our life to be forgotten for a moment. Simply the process of going through the photos and putting this book together was one way of indulging in my life with Phil, wanting to relive us, our marriage, our dreams.

The memory book I used was a large photo album with a velvet fawn colored cover and black pages on the inside. The memories commenced from the time of our meeting in 1994, and each page was filled with favourite photographs, some of the beautiful poetry that Phil had written over the years, and finally the book ended with his journey during those final months.

This included more photos, stories and emails received during this time, articles and obituaries written about Phil, readings from his funeral service and on the very last page I placed my favourite photo of Phil. It was a photo in which he was sitting in the sun shining on one side of his face. He was not facing the camera but slightly to the side, and he had the most beautiful smile in this photo. In fact I did not know that this photo existed until after his funeral. I immediately fell in love with it, and above it on the final page I wrote the words, "If ever you wanted to see what a real angel looked like."

Slowly but very meticulously I chose the contents, reminisced and shed many a tear as this book came together. Completing it was very healing for me, and by the end of the process I was able to read through the pages and feel gratitude for the memories instead of heart wrenching grief.

I was so proud of this book and felt it was a tribute to a great man. I wanted to share it with everyone. However others who had not perhaps processed and indulged in their grief as I was doing did find it difficult to read through. Whilst I had the gift of time in my grieving and had made the decision to truly feel it, others perhaps did not. It was important to remember my definition of the grieving process as a fingerprint. Whilst one could read all the books in the world and talk to others about how it was for them, ultimately we are all unique in how we pass through it and in what time frame. This was when I realized that we were all at different stages in our loss of Phil and to let others be in their process, at their own pace, just as I needed.

Zel and his wife Delwyn had planned a family trip to Croatia for his fiftieth birthday that year with their three children, Zeljana, Dominique and Xavier. Soon after Phil's funeral they invited me to go with them, and in a heartbeat the voice inside me said yes. I knew that this was an opportunity for me to live, to reach out and grasp each day of my life and experience it. After all, I had seen how short it could be. Phil would often say to me, "Tarn, life is an adventure." (He would do the craziest things.) So dear Phil, I was going to follow your advice and really live it!

Leaving Fergus was a concern for me as this small furry thing had become such an integral part of my life, and I was scared that he would wander if I was not there. He was a very social cat and loved company, so he would go searching for it. One day I had a phone call from a complete stranger who phoned me from their car as they were driving home from my area and asked if Fergus belonged to me. He had somehow made it in the back of their car and was on his way home with them!

Once I had left for my trip, Catherine told me that Fergus virtually did not move off my bed for the first two days, and for eleven days straight he brought in a bird for her. We were convinced that he must have found an aviary nearby!

The plan was to fly on my own to meet my family in Rome, board a flight together to Split, Croatia, and from there sail the Croatian coastline stopping at various islands and arriving in Dubrovnik one week later. After a few days there, we would travel by car to Medjugore, a village of pilgrimage in Bosnia where there have been reported apparitions by the Virgin Mary (or Our Lady as I refer to her) since 1981 and where to date millions of people have visited. The final stage of the holiday was to spend a few days in Paris where we would celebrate Zel's birth.

Phil and I made a pilgrimage to Medjugore in 1996 only a few months before we were married and had always dreamed of returning again. It was like finding a slice of heaven for us both. My devotion to Our Lady since that trip significantly altered for me and would be whom I would turn to during many of my personal trials including this one that was currently upon me. Ever since I was a little girl I had always felt such strength from Our Lady, women of all women, oh how I wanted to emulate her strength and courage at this time.

This holiday was certainly a turning point. I was removed from the turmoil that was inside my head and surrounding me at home. I was relaxed and had fun. I laughed a lot and enjoyed the heat. I had not really experienced the last summer at home in New Zealand. I enjoyed the children, did some shopping and I felt alive again. It was just what I needed, a reprieve from the grief.

Whilst away I found willingness within to move on with my life and there were even tinges of excitement at the thought that life for me could not only be manageable but that there would in fact be joy for me again.

I was able to accept that here I stood, alone in the world and not really attached to anything or anyone, apart from Fergus, with much of my life as I knew it now gone, and it was now time to rebuild. There was an excitement about being able to create my life in the shape I wanted it to be and had found a freedom and openness to experience what is in my life at that point in time. I knew what I had to do, to place one foot forward, and followed by the other these steps would form my own journey at my pace, and the result would be rebuilding the personal foundations of Tanya. It was just a matter of doing it.

My tank was empty, so it was the time now to refill this emptiness inside. My identity had changed. I was no longer married, not sure what direction to take with my career or any part of my life for that matter. I had to ask myself those two most difficult questions. Who was I, and where was I going?

Thursday July 14,

I feel sad leaving home. Right now I really miss him. He would have been so excited about a trip like this. I must believe that he is still excited for me. My tears are here, because I don't want to leave Phil behind which is silly. It is only his ashes that I am leaving. I had a big cry in Lois's arms when she called in to say goodbye. This is how it was meant to be. I am now at the end of this journal. My next journal will be new and fresh, perhaps a new start for me too. I am now off!

6.40 P.M. NZ time,

I am on board the flight and my sadness is here again. I think of the fact that Phil will not be with me for the rest of my life on this earth, which is why sometimes I feel that I don't want my time here to be too long.

On the other hand it does feel good to be going away. I feel so grateful for the opportunity. When I think deeply about it there is a touch of excitement about the possibilities of my life when I return. I want to find my magnificence again. Fergus should be home now. I hope that he is alright. Phil, please take care of Fergus whilst I am away.

It is vital that I relax and enjoy every part of this journey, not to miss anything or to wish it away as I have often done in my life. I want to fully feel and experience everything, and I believe that this trip will be fantastic for me if I let it be.

At the time of the holiday the children's ages were Zeljana, 22; Dominique 18 and Xavier 14. They got on superbly and whenever there was normal sibling tension it was just so funny to me. Xavier was like a battery operated boy doll that just did not stop. It was his life mission I am sure to terrorize Dominique on this journey. He wrestled, punched and was generally being a pest, which we all quietly loved about him. One of my favourite moments was taking his photo as he demonstrated his man-liness to us by placing clothes pegs on his nipples and endured the pain until I managed to find my camera and eventually take the shot.

Saturday July 16,

Here I am now on board the yacht in a village called Milina on the Adriatic coast. It is nearly ten o'clock at night and it has been a long but wonderful day. I have laughed so much today, the most in months. It is so lovely being part of this family, the dynamic is great and the children are so much fun. I feel really happy.

Most of the afternoon was spent buying provisions for the yacht and getting ready to sail. I was able to forget about my loss back home, and, whilst I kept thinking about how much Phil would have loved this, I have had reprieve from my sadness. This was great to experience, but more importantly I allowed myself to have a break from it without the guilt attached.

Our Skipper on the yacht is Borut and he is a lovely man. Zel keeps forgetting his name and is calling him everything but Borut, so he is getting a very hard time from us all. I think he has called him "borrowed," "beirut" and "borud." You name it; Zel has used it! So Borut is to sail this crazy family around the Adriatic for seven days, what an experience it will be for him.

We set sail from Split at about five-thirty in the afternoon. When we reached the open ocean and found somewhere shel-tered, we swam. Normally I would not have, but having decided to do and experience everything on this trip, I took the plunge, lit-erally! The water was beautiful and warm, and it was great to have the sun on my bare skin again. I am forgetting the horror of the past months whilst here.

It is now 2.30 A.M. I have just had four hours sleep and woken up to the sound of Croatian music. Actually it is blaring. So often something like this would upset me. I would be fretting about not getting my precious sleep but it has not. In fact, I think it is quite funny actually. This is life. The sound of the Croatian music is reminding me of when I was young and how I embraced the culture, particularly the music. I just loved it. I feel alive again.

We have moored up next to all these other boats in Milina. It is so alive but also not that private. You could eat from the plate of the person on the boat next to us. Phil you would be so getting into this right now. It makes me miss you right now. I just do! I can hear Xavier snoring in the cabin next door to me. It sounds like my father. I am not surprised he is snoring after the energy that young lad burns off during the day. It is time to sleep now.

It is now 4 A.M., and I have been awoken this time by some ladies who have just gone past, singing the Croatian song Bebo Bakuline. This is such an awesome fun song that I too want to burst into song right now. I have just got up and want to savor the moment. I want to experience my parents' culture, so who cares if I am not sleeping. This is living. I feel so grateful to be experiencing this moment.

It is early Sunday morning which is why so many are still up, walking home from the evening's festivities the night before, and some, mainly the elderly, are now also arising to work in their fields before the hot sun arises. So many of these elderly women are dressed completely in black. They are widows, like me. Blow that I say. I will not be wearing black.

The morning is cool, and I need my jersey on. How I love this time of the day. We are moored right opposite a church, and if I wasn't so scared to walk the plank on the boat I would go over and wander the main street. Another motor bike that sounds like a lawnmower has just gone past with two guys on it, neither holding the handle bar. The noise has just broken the peaceful silence that I was experiencing. But yet again it brought a smile to my face simply because I feel happy.

I have just looked up and seen the stars. Phil are you here also experiencing this?

It is so apparent to me that home alone I can become so preoccupied with my grief whereas here I am busy and I feel alive—the people and the activity. Is it good for me to stay in the grief because I feel that I should, or should I stay busy and get on with things during the day so as not to be so down? Do I allow myself to be removed from the grief? I don't know. How does one know how to grieve if there is in fact such a way? You take each day as it comes and whatever comes with it. All I know is that I am away and not consumed by pain and the most important thing is that I have given myself the permission to live without it.

Monday July 18,

It is 4.40 A.M. and I have been awake for about an hour. Yesterday was a beautiful hot day. We got up, did some shopping, stocked the boat, and off we sailed. The sun is already up. The bells have just chimed five times, and I am up on the deck with Zel sleeping up here.

Last night, being a Sunday, there was a very large procession going through the main street; it was the Feast Day of Our Lady of Mt Carmel, which is the name of the church at this village. It filled me with so much joy to watch this as so many, dedicated to their faith, singing the most beautiful hymns, proudly paraded past us all on our yachts as we sat and watched. They ranged in age from the very young to the very old, and there was no shame or embarrassment in expressing the depth of their faith and love of Our Lady. I felt such a peace in my heart at that moment—a knowing that I was being taken care of, and I was surrounded by love.

Delwyn and I went shopping and for a walk. We talked about Phil…I needed to talk about him just to get my feelings out, and then it felt better for me.

We went out to a restaurant, and I even made jokes, which was the first time in a while. It triggered me. This terrible feeling of loss came over me when I realized that Phil would not attend a meal with me again in a restaurant and have his arm on my back. He would not be back in Auckland when I got home—yet more triggers, just something that happens. The first of everything without him is very difficult. It was however, still a good night.

I walked back to the yacht early with Dominique, us two nanas needing our beauty sleep.

Tuesday July 19,

It is a Tuesday; fourteen weeks ago Phil passed away. I wonder for how long you count in weeks? I am in the cabin below. It is peaceful. Everyone is asleep, even Zel who is normally up with me at this hour. We are going to head off to Korcula today, the island where my father was born, so I suspect this will be emotional.

My reading today is about gratitude and Psalm 30—the Psalm that we got so much strength from during Phil's illness. 'Then he turned my sorrow into joy! He took away my clothes of mourning and clothed me with joy so that I might sing glad praises to the Lord instead of lying in silence in the grave.' Is this all just coincidence or do I look for signs. Is Phil now dancing?

What do I have to be grateful for? I have my good health, my faith, my good decent parents, my family, friends, Fergus and of course ten years with Phil. Experiencing a love that had no conditions attached. Phil was my gift for ten years, and I was privileged enough to have learned from him. We learned from each other.

Today has been a fun day. What this trip has done for me is enabled me to chill out and take risks such as rowing by myself out in the ocean, swimming with the girls in the ocean when once upon a time I would have been fearful of joy.

One of the techniques both Phil and I used was something we called a Gratitude Journal. We both kept one during his illness, although I was not as vigilant in keeping it up to date as Phil was. Every night Phil would place at least six things in his journal that he had to be grateful for. I commenced my own gratitude journal pretty much as soon as Phil passed away, a small but pretty notebook into which daily I placed all of the things in my life that I had to be grateful for.

This tool would often begin my shift in mood and take me out of my dark moments; I would always find something, even if it was something minor, that made me laugh that day. It enabled me to remember that no matter how bad life seemed for me, deep down I knew there was always something that I could be positive about and that soon joy would follow.

I discovered that my greatest task was to appreciate the joy when it was with me and not expect or wait for it to be taken away.

Wednesday July 20,

Here we are in Racisce, on the Island of Korcula and the birthplace of my father. It is 5 A.M. and already people are up in the village. Yesterday was exciting as we sailed in at about three o'clock. It was even more so seeing Zel's joy as he saw dads home emerging. We stood at the front of the yacht, no doubt all of us feeling some emotion, especially watching Zel. Of course Xavier was making us all laugh as he performed and swung from the ropes like a monkey!

We moored on a jetty, and the kids were all jumping off the side of the boat into the beautiful clear water. Zel, Delwyn and I went to the house where my father was raised. It brought back memories for me of my trip here in 1981 with my parents and staying in this very house. I reflected on my dad, his difficult life and what he and my mom endured in their lives and sacrificed for their children by leaving their family and coming to a foreign country. In spite of their many trials they remain so faithful to the Lord. Once again, I felt grateful.

What I have loved about this trip is getting to know the kids, being a part of this family and feeling a sense of belonging.

It is now nearly midnight, and I have awoken feeling such terrible guilt that I am so happy. I am busy, preoccupied. The grief is not smashing me so much, and I am feeling real joy! Who says that I have to be miserable all of the time? It is important to allow myself happiness again. Besides, how long does one grieve for anyway?

It is great having no stress in my life. I really have been able to let go and enjoy this trip, to forget about my reality at home.

When I return home it will be time for me to start putting my life together. I feel recharged.

The next few days we sailed our way back to Dubrovnik via other beautiful islands such as Hvar and during the day having stops at various bays to have lunch, to swim and walk and finally mooring for our final night at sea at the tiniest secluded bay. It was certainly a destination that only a skipper who had sailed these seas countless times before would know of—including the good food that one could get at the local (and only) restaurant.

There was not a lot to do at this bay, apart from watching Zel, Borut and Xavier sit in the tavern feeding themselves on the delicacies that had been prepared for them by the chef and enjoying the red wine of course. The setting was not quite up to standard for us girls so we stayed on board and watched them, ate whatever provisions were on the yacht and endured a non-appetizing sight of the German tourists who frolicked naked on the yacht next to us. It actually was very funny and was all it took for us girls to be entertained that evening.

After enjoying a few days in Dubrovnik, we collected a rental van and made our way to Medjugore, Bosnia which was only a two hour drive away. I was incredibly excited about going there and could barely contain my joy that morning. Perhaps I felt I would be closer to Our Lady there, or to Phil. Perhaps I thought that this little piece of heaven for me would be where I would find the peace I was longing for.

Driving into the village and seeing the familiar sight of the church that was surrounded by the hills was like falling into a very comfortable couch, one where I could lay and just relax, feeling as though I had not a care in the world. I was there to pray, to reflect, to be silent, to surrender to my God and ask that somehow my own heart could now be at peace.

The first afternoon we all made our way up Mount Podbora known as the Hill of Apparitions which is the site of the first apparition back in 1981. Climbing this hill, each decade of the rosary was represented by a large upstanding plaque where we could quietly reflect on the meaning of Christ's life.

This climb led us to the final place of reflection where the most beautiful statue of Our Lady stands at the actual site of the apparition. Whilst I had been there before, and prayed at this same spot with Phil all those years earlier, somehow there was a greater beauty for me about this white statue. Perhaps it was the peace that had infiltrated my heart during the climb and now, coming to this place of solitude.

As Phil lay in his open casket at home one morning I quietly went in and cut a lock of his hair. Well truthfully, it was a considerable chunk which I carefully snipped from the back of his head so that it was not too noticeable. Phil was very proud of his thick hair, and I am sure he would have found this very amusing. I was not yet sure what I would do with it at the time. I just knew to take some. Well, when leaving for the trip to Europe I knew to take some of his hair to Medjugore and to scatter it there. I was not sure exactly where I would drop some of these locks of his hair, but once I reached the top of the Hill of Apparitions and stood at this statue, I knew deep inside that this was where it must be done.

By chance I carried his hair with me so at that point I reached into my pocket and pulled out the small white container and held it in my clasped hands for a moment. I opened the lid and my tears began as I held out my hand for each of my family to remove a small lock of Phil's hair so that we could each take part in this small ritual.

In our own time each of us released a small physical part of Phil at the site which he so loved, his heaven on earth. My tears began to gently fall as I let go of what remained in my little container and I felt at peace, however it was when I heard the word *goodbye* twice in my heart that I fell apart. It felt as though my chest opened up, and the pain that emerged from the tear it created was unbearable. "How can I say goodbye to you," I said. I began to cry from the depths of my soul as I slowly walked away from the crowd. It had only then occurred to me that I had not said goodbye to Phil when he was dying. Neither of us had uttered those words that night on April 12.

As Phil was taking his final breaths, perhaps I did not believe that this would be goodbye. All I wanted to do was to keep holding him and telling him that I loved him, but not goodbye. It was that afternoon at that tiny village in Bosnia which represented heaven on earth for me. I said goodbye to my husband, whom I believe was looking down upon me from

Heaven itself. What I now needed was to take home with me this feeling of heaven on earth. It had to be within me.

That night in our room Zeljana, who was also my goddaughter and twenty years younger than me, lay my head on her lap as she gentled massaged my temples. I was emotionally exhausted and it was she who nurtured her Teta (Auntie) Tanya that night.

The following morning I awoke early. I knew that the church would be open all night for those who wanted to keep a vigil. I had the desire to be there as soon as I could. At 4.30 A.M. I was sitting in a pew in this very large church, which at this early hour was almost full.

The only light inside the church was that generated by candles lit around the edges of the altar and the side aisles which created softness to the crisp morning air. We were all strangers in the church that morning, gathered from every corner of the earth and with our own private intentions. However I felt as though there was a common bond between us all. It was of the faith that we shared and our belief of the phenomenon which was happening in this village during our times. For myself, it was the search for a greater peace and acceptance of what had occurred in my life and to obtain a greater trust in what was yet to come.

Once again I prayed the familiar prayer to my God and Our Lady that somehow I find my purpose in life and to have the strength and willingness to carry it out. I needed to know that Phil was alright, at peace and in Heaven. In spite of the depth of my faith, I still needed to be shown and how I was to be shown I did not know.

By the time I left the church the sun had come through from behind the mountains and I noticed how the village was already becoming busier with the locals commencing their daily routines. As I walked to the right of the church I found an enclosed area where you could light candles for your intentions and leave them burning as you sat and prayed or reflected. At the entrance of this beautiful setting was a very large wooden cross that stood approximately four meters high.

That morning I had candles burning for everything and everyone, and once they were lit I began to pray. As I did I looked up and noticed two white doves perched at the very top of this tall wooden cross. They were just nibbling at each other and immediately I thought of Phil as he loved doves and often said to me that when he meditated he would often think of doves which for him signified peace. Once again I just kept looking for a sign that Phil was at peace and what I chose to believe was that this may have been a sign.

The other hill that surrounded the village of Medjugore was Mt Kricevac, or Cross Mountain. At its very top was an enormous concrete cross which was erected by the locals in 1933. Late that afternoon we headed out for the arduous climb up Mt Kricevac. There was no easy path on this climb. It was nothing but dirt and rocks all the way up. Many make this climb in their bare feet as a form of sacrifice, however we all donned our runners and still moaned about the discomfort of the heat.

It is on this climb that you reflect on the Stations of the Cross, the Passion of Christ on Good Friday and the heaviness of the cross He carried for us. My continuous prayer, as we climbed in the heat of the afternoon, was "Lord, Your cross too was heavy. Thank You for helping me to carry my cross in this lifetime." It was still so soon after Phil's death, and to me it felt like a very heavy cross for me to bare. I was still unsure of how I would endure it. The climb certainly gave you time to reflect on your life and to also count your blessings.

We had only one day left in Medjugore, and I wanted to be up at dawn to savor this time in my little slice of heaven and one more time to light more candles before we left that morning. Phil had candles burning for him in every church that I had entered into during our stay in Croatia, and there was the need to do it again this morning.

I ignited enough candles that morning to heat the entire village as one final assurance I had covered all bases that Phil was fine and to ensure that all of my friends and family had candles burning for them, not to mention myself. I prayed for the willingness to live on and to find my blessings every day and remember everything I had to be grateful for, which was plenty.

As I stood in silence looking up at that large wooden cross, once again two white doves flew along and perched themselves at the very top and began to nibble at each other. At that moment I needed to hear nothing else. My heart was at peace; Phil was happy, of that I was sure, and I had no doubt that I too would be happy. This for me was another sign.

Later that morning we left Medjugore and spent some time with my mother's family in a small village called Opuzen. Then we slowly made our way up the Croatian Coast toward Split, admiring the magnificent views as we drove north and passed each village tucked into the coastline. Zel, driving the van, kept us rather amused as each time he saw a spectacular sight he made the same comment in the most innocent, childlike voice, "Would you look at that," he would say. As you can imagine, soon we were either imitating him or responding in a way that had some form of cheek attached to it, as if he cared. It was a fun journey north.

July 30, Paris, France,

Here I am, and my final day of sleep in Europe is over. Yesterday was a great day. It was filled with some sightseeing, shopping and finally dinner out to celebrate Zel's birthday.

Getting dressed up again to go out to dinner was fun. I had not done that for some time. The restaurant was very fancy. The food was presented beautifully and tasted even better. Dominique and I horrified the waiter when we sent our lamb back asking that it be cooked a bit more—probably not what you do in a classy restaurant in Paris! Oh well.

What I was aware of was not having Phil with me in Paris, a city where you are to be with someone whom you love. Thankfully however I still had a great time. Anyway, I believe that he has seen it all by now, he has seen Paris and all of the other amazing things on our trip.

July 31,

Now we are on board the flight to Auckland, yeah! I am so excited. I have just had a twelve hour flight from Paris to Singapore, and I slept most of the way. I feel great now, and I am really looking forward to getting home and getting started with my life.

There is no doubt in my mind that Phil is absolutely fine and in a far greater place, very happy in fact. It was so important for me to have this deep knowing, because I still was not quite sure.

It is now up to me to continue on in life without him. And one day at a time I feel I can do this.

I absolutely loved this trip; it reminded me of my love of travel. I feel a zest for life which I have not experienced before since I did not allow it for myself. I was unable to step out of the self imposed roles and restrictions that I had created for myself, of not allowing myself to be me, to discover me, to feel joy or to be happy in case it was taken from me. This has now been a real gift for which I am so grateful.

Phil's passing has been my greatest trauma. It has however enabled me to experience what I believe is the greatest gift I—to be present as your loved one passed from this life onto the next stage, to be there as they surrendered themselves to God. As painful as this is, I would do it all again in a heartbeat for you Phil. In fact I can now see how these early experiences of such grief so soon in my life, firstly with dad's cancer, then with mom's and now of course with my precious Phil, will be part of me for the rest of my life. It now feels perfectly fine for me to live on.

There seems to be more of an acceptance of this entire journey, his and mine, and it was he who had to make the decisions concerning his body. I had to support him and trust the correct decisions were made for him as he wanted. Phil's decisions were perfect. He was staunch, and even up until that last week he prayed for a miracle and wanted to recover naturally. He trusted so much in God. He trusted so much that it was the will of God to heal him physically, but it was a spiritual healing that was taking place the entire time.

My grief about Phil has changed somehow, and my life feels manageable right now. Whilst there is some concern about my future, I also know that I have what it takes to have a meaningful and purposeful life, which in time I will really discover. I am really excited about getting home and seeing Fergus, and I no longer wish for my life to be over but am grateful that I am alive.

THIRTEEN

Home to Discover Me

During the previous weeks, whilst removed from my home environment and the daily reminders of my loss, I had made a decision to move forward and felt very excited about the possibilities for my life. I did however want it to happen at an accelerated pace and continued to place far too much in my life and on my plate. Perhaps I was hoping to skip over some of the grief and pain that I knew was still inevitable.

Even though I had made the decision to move forward with my life, I was aware that this nightmare would not simply magically disappear. Being busy did help and it felt as though at least I was doing something tangible towards building my future and once again discovering my purpose in being here after all.

Therefore along with the darkness and cold of the winter days, also came the darkness and anxiety about my future. In spite of feeling so positive upon my return from our holiday, once home and on my own again, my moods began to sway daily. Like an unsettled ocean, they would move from a feeling of peace within and of absolute trust that my life would be a good one, to a feeling of overwhelming doubt and anxiety.

My anger periodically continued to surface and often I was not sure at what. The emotional drain that this created would often throw me off balance. Often I would internalize this anger so as not to direct it elsewhere. Anger was not an emotion I displayed often in my life. My belief was that it was not appropriate to do so. Yet here it was—this very realistic emotion of anger building inside me. I was often unaware of how to handle it or where to direct it or at whom.

I was looking forward to commencing work and building my business again. Life needed to go on, and I felt a real willingness to do this, so when it naturally began to happen I was thrilled.

Upon my return quite a lot of computer work just flooded in for me, which took me by surprise. I had not spent a lot of time on that part of my career to date, so I decided to just go with it and to trust that this was what I was meant to be doing at the time. This proved to be very beneficial for me. The mental stimulation was exactly what I needed, and mixing with my clients, many of whom were friends, was a breath of fresh air. The conversation was not always about me and my circumstances, which I believe kept me stuck in the grief, but it was about others and work related issues. It was a breath of fresh air for me to also leave my home on a daily basis. I was becoming rather reclusive during the cold winter days.

After three months of not having a dining room suite in my lounge (because I did not want to have to sit at a dinner table on my own) I finally went out and invested in one. I was now ready to eat at the table again and willing to start entertaining again, which is something that I had always loved doing.

My table arrived, but to my horror, in many pieces. I found it interesting how it was often minor issues that would tip me over the edge as far as stress goes. The thought of working out how to put this table together caused me much distress. I believe it was yet another reminder of Phil's absence. It was time to learn new skills. Admittedly, once the task was accomplished with the assistance of good friends, there was a level of satisfaction that I had achieved something.

In 2001 I decided to alter the course of my career and commenced my studies towards a Diploma in Counseling. This proved to be a life transforming event for me. It enabled me to work through many of my own life issues and to deal deeply with my grief around not having my own children.

I loved to be in the helping profession, and in the August after Phil's death again I extended my studies to Life and Corporate Coaching and enrolled in an extensive course which I commenced the following month.

These were all things that I believed would add to my repertoire of skills. I wanted to learn, to soak up as much knowledge as I could. This was one way of taking action to then see where my path would lead me, since I was still uncertain.

To balance out the additional studies and work, I recommenced my early morning swimming sessions. I remember my first swim. it was so wonderful to see my friends again, and the feeling of passing through the water was invigorating. There was such a freedom in the movement and a feeling as though I was being cleansed of the pain. There was no pressure on my body as each stroke forward for me in the water was like stepping forward with my life, reaching out to my new being. I was never a fast swimmer, and being at the back of the slow lane was not an issue for me at all!

The other creative activity I recommenced was to sew my own clothing, something I had always loved to do in my spare time. What I found interesting was that the fabrics I had chosen were of the brightest colors. To me they made a statement to the world, perhaps that I was alive. Wearing black was not an option at this time. It reminded me of Phil's funeral, and it signified darkness, not life.

In fact my aunt in Croatia asked if when I returned for my holiday if I would be wearing black. So many of the young widows in Croatia still do. Well, I assured my auntie that I would make sure that in my suitcase would be packed a tiny black bikini, which would be the extent of my mourning clothes.

At times I had to force myself out the door to swim or to my sewing classes. However, once I was there, it was the best medication for me. I realized that one of the quickest ways to rise up when I was feeling down was to actually get moving, albeit, sometimes not that quickly. Sometimes it was just to physically remove myself from the four walls that were becoming so familiar to me. Once I actually took action to move my body, or any other behavioral action, my thinking and feelings would shift in a positive way along with my body.

The lows still came in strong and fast, my *tsunamis* as I referred to them, and on occasion, in order to remove myself from the pain on some level, my comfort eating and excessive thinking about my body size would take over. This I was aware of, and sometimes I would just say "OK, if this is what I have to do for now then so be it."

Phil's little room was still covered with photos and memorabilia. Now however, it felt time to start putting some things away since I believe this kept me in the depths of my grief. There was no guilt attached to this for me, and whilst I was not sure how much or what I would put away, the important fact was the real desire within, for me to now commence moving on.

Tuesday August 2, 3.15 A.M.,

It is now sixteen weeks since Phil passed away. Fergus is on the bed with me and very happy that I am home. I cannot sleep. I am jetlagged and thinking about how hard it is being alone. God made Adam *and* Eve for a reason!

I woke up thinking of Phil as I was dreaming of him. He was crying and told me that people at Foodtown said he was doing the wrong thing, that he should have done chemotherapy. He did what felt right for him, and I believe it was the right decision. Nothing could have spared him from this beast. For some reason I need to document all of my dreams about Phil. I am not sure why, a bit like keeping a memory of him I suppose.

Today has been a good day. I went to sewing again which has once again fuelled my creative side, and I thoroughly enjoyed it. Work is coming in, and I was busy in my office, so that has also motivated me.

Tiredness changes my thinking and gets me fearful, hence I must be sure that I sleep, or even just rest.

Finally I feel excited about my plans and my life, however on some level I also feel guilty for feeling this way. Am I feeling happy too soon? When can I start to show the world that I am excited about my future again? Somehow I feel a freedom to move forward with my dreams again, more so than I did before. It was as if I did not allow myself to discover my true self before. Something kept me stuck. Perhaps it was I who kept me stuck.

Saturday August 6, 7.30 A.M.,

Today has been a bit tough. I was indecisive with everything, overwhelmed at what to do in my day. My head was spinning. There was so much I wanted to do but just did not know where to start. I was running and even disorganized. Why have I placed such restrictions on myself? There is no need for it. Is this all part of trying to be in control of my life, or even in control of my grieving process?

Today I had tears, because I missed Phil and my heart aches at the thought of not having him with me, what a cross to carry. Prayer helps me and is one of the things that provide me with real peace at this time.

Tonight there came clarity in my life about my career. It was to commence business again—to commence it now in fact, to move further into helping others. That was very clear to me and is what I feel passionate about.

Sunday August 7, 6.20 A.M.,

I am now in bed with Fergus lying on my chest staring at me. This is great. I enjoy him when he is like this. What a sad state of affairs when a cat is giving you emotional support, but the little beggar does!

How different I feel in the mornings and even an excitement about my life, especially, after a good sleep. It is therefore important to plan things for the afternoons when I am more fatigued. That is my tough time. I need to eat well during the day, not foods that bring my blood sugar to a slump. That also can affect my moods. Grief is hideous enough as it is without taking care of me, therefore if I can do practical things to compensate some of the tough times then I need to.

Slowly I feel as though I have the energy to start doing things, to start living again. Tonight I was making plans for my business and life, which all felt good, really uplifting in fact.

One of the tools I used to motivate myself with my life and future was to create a dream board. I purchased a large piece of colored paper, and on it I placed all of the things that I wished for myself in my life, all of which were made up mainly of cutouts from magazines, pictures, words, and phrases.

At the very top I placed a photograph of Phil and myself on my fortieth birthday. It was a photo where I was looking away from him and he was slightly behind and was looking over me. This photo signified to me that, whilst we were together in a sense, he was more like an angel looking over me. Underneath this photo I placed a cutout with the words, "Don't be afraid."

Some of the pictures that I placed on my board were of holiday destinations that I would like to go to, pictures of clothing and shoes (of course), beautiful foods, lovely home décor and a new car. Motivating words and phrases that I placed on my dream board were, "Feel Like," "Iron Woman," "Calm and Coping," "A Future," "It feels like the right thing for my body," "How to be a great leader" and "Home comforts."

This large piece of pink board remained up in my bedroom so that I was able to see it as I lay in my bed and as a reminder of what was possible in my life. If I focused on what I now wanted in my life, then it would come to me. I began to think abundantly on all levels, emotionally, spiritually, intellectually and physically. As I write this now, I am able to say that some of these images placed on my board have already come to fruition one way or another. Phil and I created one of these boards during his illness. This one, however, was now different.

In addition to the dream board I also bought an artist's sketch block, A3 in size, which was my vision/goals book, and each page had a different theme. The very first page was a list of everything that gave me joy in my life at that time. For example, it included my quiet time in the morning, all of my creative activities, what was present in my work and study life and what sort of social activities were in my life. Most importantly I listed all of the ways that I nurtured myself on a daily basis: with good nutritious foods, kindness towards myself, the exercise that I was doing in my week and other basic self care. In fact, I dedicated the entire second page to self care activities and where they were placed in my day and week.

The third page was entitled, "My Life Goals and Dreams." The very first entry on this page read, "To make a difference in the lives of others and humanity." Other entries related to my career ambitions, my continuing education ambitions, my travel desires, my exercise goals and my desire to write a book one day and reach others with my message and the story that Phil wanted to tell.

It was a dream to once again return to Medjugore for a pilgrimage and also once again to ski on a United States ski slope, which I had not done for many years. It was important that I document all of my dreams as this was all part of building my future and knowing deeply that these were all within reach some day. These tasks all gave me hope.

The next five pages were detailed ways of how I would develop myself on certain levels, namely, Spiritually, Emotionally, Physically, Creatively and Career. My career page was even more specific as to the type of work I wanted to incorporate in my private practice. I was very specific in everything that I wanted to accomplish and ways that I could achieve them and what tools and resources were available to me.

My next page was a list of all of the books that I had read either fully or partly which had an influence on my personal journey and those which I would be using as resources in my work with others.

Next was a time line, horizontally placed on the page, from the years 2005–2007. Each year was placed evenly on the top, and below I wrote down the goals that I wanted to achieve in specific time frames. Only those goals that were measurable and realistic were placed on this time line, such as additional studies, financial goals, holiday goals and even some creative goals.

Being a rather visual person, doing the time line was very motivating for me. It was encouraging for me to move forward with clear goals that were very specific and achievable, rather than just dreams.

The next pages were dedicated at looking at the possible obstacles that could get in the way of achieving some of the things in my vision that I had created on the pages prior. I asked myself questions and answered them in the most honest way that I could. After all, these pages were for my eyes only, so I was able to be brutally honest with myself. Some of the questions that I asked myself on these pages were: What single change can I make that will have the biggest impact on my personal and professional life? What are the most important things in my life, and what do I do to nurture them? What could stand in the way of me achieving my dreams and goals?

Wednesday August 10,

My day started tough without a good sleep. I didn't exercise. I went to Mass instead. The traffic got me angry, and then I came home to a dead bird thanks to Fergus! My day felt nuts. I got home then had a stressful night trying to get this wretched lounge suite together. Thank God for Ursula and Leanne. I am now tired and drained, but it feels great to know that I got through the day without comfort—eating or losing it with tears. Lord, help me to slow down.

It is such a relief to actually know and experience that no matter how bad you feel, these feelings do pass and all you have to do is go through them. Attempts to escape them one way or another leads to more pain. Just sit and be with these feelings and get up and just do it. Do whatever needs to be done to ride it out.

Thursday August 11,

Tonight I feel tired and stressed and need peace and quiet. The dining room incident really upset me, as did having so many visitors today. It is vital to remember that often when there is so much pain lingering, it is the little things that can so easily tip you over. You are often not thinking rationally when you are overwhelmed, hence, having a messy lounge and not seeing past it was all it took for me to lose it today.

I place a lot of demands on myself, and I want to escape these demands. It all takes so much energy. I have a real desire to move forward with my life and not to sit around and have coffee with so many who so kindly want to visit me or see me. Perhaps I should be grateful, but I don't have the energy to talk any more. It is getting to the point now where I find my phone ringing intolerable. I need to be left alone for now.

Once again so much is about learning personal boundaries. I am drained and need to speak about uplifting things now and not so much about Phil's death. Perhaps this too is part of the grieving process.

On a good note, today I got up early at 4.45 A.M., and I had a swim with the squad for the first time since last October, and I absolutely loved it. It was great being back in the pool and seeing people again. I felt alive and free moving through the water, as if I was slowly moving through my life again. It was such a wonderful healing feeling.

Tuesday August 16,

Well, after such a peaceful day yesterday, another tsunami of grief hit today. You just don't quite know when you will get hit with one. I can fill up my life with everything, but I still don't have Phil. That is the long and short of it. My heart is yearning for him right now. Is this what all the busyness and planning is about—filling up my life? How can this void in my life of not having you here Phil, be filled? Help me please to daily do what it takes to get through and not try to run from this hideous pain when it comes. It seems too good to be true when a good day comes. You think, yeah, this is over. Then wham you get slammed again. There is not a reason why; it just hits.

Sometimes I feel so guilty over what I am not doing, which means I don't enjoy what I am doing in the present moment. At the moment I am thinking that I should be doing all this stuff, seeing all these people, when in fact I need to remember what I have just gone through and not to put too much pressure on myself. It is as if I think that my grieving should be perfect also.

What is the use of setting such high expectations for myself when really it just sets me up if I don't achieve them?

Thursday August 18,

At the moment my faith is not an option—but a matter of life and death. This is how it feels for me right now. One day at a time, it is about holding onto my faith, letting go and trusting. I don't quite know how else to get through at the moment.

There is so much guilt surrounding me at the moment. Is this what survivor's guilt is all about, that I cannot begin to enjoy my life, because I am alive and Phil is not?

Now that I have come down off the high that I was on upon returning home from holiday I have realized that this transition that I am wanting will not happen in a flash. Part of my journey through this grieving process is to slow down and fill in the gaps, particularly this big empty space of being alone in the world. It is about filling it up with healthy things that will nurture me on a physical, emotional, spiritual and intellectual level, not unnecessary busyness which tires me.

These things I must be passionate about first and foremost, even things to step out of my comfort zone with. It is also vital that I must do what it takes to feel the pain of my loss. I know logically that once that tsunami has passed, I am able to pick myself up again and rise up to life.

Sunday August 21,

What a great day, such a difference for me to put my quiet time and prayer first in my day. I cleaned up Phil's room. It felt timely to put away some of the not so important bits of his memorabilia. No longer do I feel as though I have to place everything of Phil up just in case I might forget him. There is willingness to move ahead and slowly let go of this need to stay connected at this level.

Life can get quite lonely being on your own, however being alone is what I want a lot of the time, and I enjoy just being inside during these winter months. It is during these lonely times that I am slowly finding out about myself and becoming aware of my own potential in the world. Something was always stopping me, both internally and externally, from allowing myself to reach this potential and really seeing my own magnificence, a magnificence that exists in us all. Now is the time to discover it and release it.

So often in my earlier years it was low self worth and not feeling worthy of joy which kept me from stepping out of my comfort zone.

Wednesday August 24,

It is now 3.30 A.M. I don't know why, but I often awake during the night. In fact I have now been awake for over two hours and it feels unbearable. What is doing this to me? Am I now becoming too impulsive about doing everything, not missing out? Do I now feel that life is so short that I must do everything this year, this week? Am I being too busy and trying to run from pain?

It is now the evening, and today I had a great day. Can you believe it? I feel great now, and in fact I cannot believe how well I have coped today, considering I felt so insane during the night when I could not sleep. I really had to put my tools into action, and today I knew to halt and to do everything to get through my day."

Halt stands for Hungry, Angry, Lonely or Tired. Whenever I felt vulnerable or perhaps when my moods were low, I would ask myself if I was in one of those states. More often than not I would be. Often it was simple sadness that may have been crippling me at the time. I became aware and knew that I had to halt and take steps to prevent myself from going down any further. At times all I had to do was to give myself permission to not do anything else for the rest of the day. This in itself would relieve my pressure to *do*, and simply allow me to sit and just *be*.

More often than not, it was a simple need for some self care which would then turn my mood or irrational thinking around, and my day could proceed as originally planned.

FOURTEEN

Avoidance, Processing, Letting Go

The early months of spring seemed to be a time of deep reflection for me. Whilst my moods were still very changeable, there did not seem to be the depth of the lows that I had experienced in the previous months. In fact, often I felt unusual highs and excitement as I began to think of the possibilities of my future.

The sound of the early morning Spring birds would often spark this excitement for me as I sat in my quiet room during those early hours when I would awaken. There would be glimpses of joy at the thought of the changing seasons and the longer days.

The onset of spring would take me back into reminiscing as to what was happening that time the previous year, or the memories of particular events during that season. It was during this early morning time that I indulged in my journaling—my friend and confidant, my means of expressing my feelings, someone whom I could talk to but did not need to listen to. It was a means by which to express whatever was going on for me, no matter how insane I felt things were for me at the time. Getting it out of my head and onto paper was vital and an integral part of my healing.

Much of my journaling was an outpouring of prayer. It was one way that I would talk to God, and now it became the most valuable part of my day. It prepared me somehow for whatever my day would bring. Slowly I was becoming more able to sit and be with myself for longer periods of time, and, whilst I found this incredibly difficult, it was becoming very apparent to me that somehow I needed to quiet my being, to stop the excessive doing and thinking, which was now exhausting for me.

The consequence of this stillness was loneliness, which I was now experiencing more of, and I knew was inevitable, so it became a double edged sword at times. I so desperately wanted the quiet and to be alone with myself, yet it meant learning also to be alone with myself and to truly get to know who Tanya was.

My faith grew to a deeper level. I listened more, asked more, and was willing to receive more. Finally I was willing to pick myself up and move forward with my life, knowing that the closer I remained to my God, the more comfort I would receive whilst on my journey. It was at this point I was beginning to move into the deeper search for whom I was and what my purpose in this life was to be from now on.

Once again I delved into my creative side, and I soon realized that expressing myself through this means was yet another avenue of healing. It was during this time that I became motivated to write this book. I was not sure how or where the writing would take me. I just knew that it had to be written, and now was the time to commence.

It was important that I be aware of my motive in writing this book and to ensure it was simply not a healing task for me but something with a greater purpose. I commenced writing the book that spring. The feelings this brought up however proved to be too real and painful for me. As I wrote about the night Phil was diagnosed, I could not continue, and it was not until one year later, the following September, nearly to the day in fact, that the words would begin to flow.

Friday September 2,

I have had an awesome day. Free of all pain today. Thank You God and my angel Phil. Prayer really works. Yesterday was dad's birthday and we all went out to dinner as a family, a good night out for all tonight. It brought home how I really miss going out to dinners and having a social life, but this will change one day when I am ready. It still feels rather strange going out on my own as a single woman. I feel rather exposed, as if everyone is looking at me wondering why I am alone. I still wear my wedding rings but have no one at my side as proof that a husband exists."

Sunday September 4,

I am now in Phil's room and wanting to pray, but I feel the pain. I have just allowed my tears to come. Sometimes I just do not understand. All I must do is to accept what is.

This time of year is difficult. It used to be so joyous for me once. As I felt spring coming on, all of the signs of spring would bring such joy for me—the early morning light and of course the sounds of the birds. Two days ago I felt joyous, yet down I come again.

I continue to awake a lot during the night, however, it is getting better. It is not torment when I awake. It is simply a split second of not knowing, then realizing this is all true and that Phil is gone and that now I need to be strong myself to get through this life.

Wednesday September 7,

This morning I feel vulnerable. I have been up since 3.30 A.M., and I am so tired. I could quite easily eat sugary food to keep me awake. This is a time when I have to *halt*. I feel tired and lonely, so I have given myself permission to do absolutely nothing else today if that is what I have to do in order to get through my day.

I am really feeling the aloneness at the moment. I don't have much going on, and I am spending a lot of time on my own so I am really feeling this pain, which is good though since I am not running from it either.

What I believe is happening is that I am not comatose by excess sugar, and this space has emerged—these feelings, the pain, the realities, the opportunities, the uncertainties. They have all arisen now. I don't seem to need as much sleep either when my diet is good, therefore I have extra time to fill in my day now. How will I do that?

I will give myself to the end of the year to consolidate things, to let go and see what happens, to be creative, just do whatever is put in front of me and to really get myself together, if such a thing exists and to get my home sorted.

At this present moment I feel the need to draw what is in my heart.

In my journal I then proceeded to draw two pictures of myself. The one on the left hand page was me with a very sad face, and I wrote, "Me not moving forward, dull my pain, running from life." I drew my hair curly as it was when I was a little girl and wrote that it signified my insides being foggy and not clear. The words I wrote were that I am not fully present with myself or others and that I remove myself from the intimacy of life and relationships.

On the right hand side of the page I drew myself happy and feeling as though I was moving forward and nurturing myself properly. I was smiling, and I had a beautiful feminine dress on and wearing my amethyst which was shining, as was my face. Some of the words that I used to describe myself in my picture were: "business woman, strong, free, clear headed, courageous, brave, kind, giving, loving, to serve others, confident, mastery, athletic, happy, creative, responsible, patient, at peace, centered," and "free." Why would I want to be this other person, filled with sadness and pain? How would it serve me in my life? Actually it would not.

Sunday September 11,

For some strange reason this morning I awoke to the thought of a new relationship and how difficult that would be, the logistics of it all, no way. The loss of Phil is the greatest loss. You then think of the loss of everything else attached to that, what a mountain. When I consider what a chore to have to rebuild that again with someone else, I ask myself why on earth I would?

It is now the evening, and I am now in Phil's room with Fergus who is loving me heaps and wanting heaps of cuddles right now. What a joy this is. Having him does relieve some of the loneliness. He has such an awesome personality.

Today has been a brilliant day—really letting go of the small stuff and moving forward with a positive attitude. What a difference that in itself makes, having an attitude of gratitude.

What was also significant for me was that I prayed for the willingness to let go of the trauma of Phil's final month, and particularly those final hours and final breaths. In spite of these moments being so painful for me, for some reason I have not been willing to let them go since his death. Perhaps it has been my way of wanting to stay connected to Phil and not let him go. Today I was finally willing, and it was this willingness, in my own time, which has been the key to letting go. I asked Phil to help me with that today, and sure enough the freedom which followed has come instantly.

Another significant change for me today was that I was able to speak with and pray to Phil today without the tears which often accompanied my contact with him. Whilst there is still incredible disbelief that he is gone, that this has happened in my life somehow today, indicates something has shifted for me.

Tonight I feel great and happy even. I believe that is what he wants for me, to be happy. What would I want for him? All of that, of course, and then some.

Wednesday September 14,

How can this be that I am feeling so good?

What is so apparent to me today is how much I am helped spiritually. I feel as though there is nothing that I should truly fear or be concerned about. I can trust completely that all is well in my world. What a wonderful place I am in when I let go and pray for guidance from God.

It feels as though I am passing through something, as though something major is going on with me. Perhaps I am letting go or moving forward, whatever that means.

I have recognized my difficulty to just sit and be. I always have to be moving, whether exercising, housework, working, or studying, so now I have decided to give myself permission to sit and do nothing if that is what I chose.

All things are possible for me. I refuse to feel sorry for myself. I am very aware of my aloneness, yes, and I must admit that I do feel lonely. I have decided however that this is going to be an opportunity for me to grow.

Anger has always been an emotion which I was conditioned to believe was not appropriate to be expressed, and whilst growing up, one of the ways that I kept any anger from arising or being shown, was to comfort eat. As a result any such emotion was therefore internalized and not fully expressed.

As I became more comfortable to simply sit and be more fully present with my feelings, slowly the boil was beginning to erupt in me and finally the anger about Phil's death and my situation had arrived. Slowly the anger began to seep through, and thankfully I recognized it and allowed it to surface from within where it had been trapped for many months.

The boil eventually burst and this outpouring of anger seemed to appear at the most unusual times and during the most unusual situations. It took me by surprise that the full extent of my anger had only just arrived after what I had perceived as acceptance of my life and situation and even whilst experiencing a willingness to move forward.

The challenge for me now was to express it, to allow this strong emotion of anger to arise and let it out without chastising myself for doing so, because it was often perceived as a negative emotion.

As a result I was then able to recognize that whenever my busyness would return, or I wanted to escape on some level, it was probably the anger that I was attempting to run from. All I had to do was to keep peeling back the layers to get to the core of my feelings, and often underneath the anger was pure and simple sadness.

Sunday September 25, 4.15 A.M.,
I am feeling my loss again, and the loneliness is very much there—not sharing my life with others and myself with someone. I have too much love to give. Where can I direct some of this love I wonder? Perhaps some of it could go to my nieces and nephews. Perhaps into my clients is where a lot of my love will go. The

thought of a future alone is daunting at times, however, I must continue to trust and go within.

All of a sudden anger is beginning to appear, anger I believe that I have kept silent all of these months, perhaps by not feeling that I was allowed to be angry, especially not at God. Yesterday my cell phone landed in the water, so that upset me, and it seems that everyone is making me angry and getting in my way. I have felt a bit emotional at the loss of Phil and the safety of my marriage. Having to be in the big wide world on my own feels rather scary for me.

I feel really sad that everything is so different. There are so many losses, and yes I feel pretty angry about the whole thing all of a sudden. I did not deserve this hand.

Now here I am left wondering what my purpose is, my reason for living. With no children to live for, it is very difficult to see my reason for being here.....What is the point? What is very much with me is how my life is now and how it will be from now on. Right now this is all about me and how tough it is for me. I will allow this self pity for a bit I think!

Wednesday September 28,

It is 2.15 A.M. and I have just woken up from a dream. This dream felt like Phil was here, and I heard his voice say to me *I love you* as I awoke from this dream. I feel so much pain right now. This is such hideous pain, and I foolishly thought over the past weeks that as I was feeling so good then perhaps the bad stuff was over, but here it is again. Right now I am saying, why me; why am I the one to have to endure such pain and suffering in my life? I am so angry!

Today I feel very teary. My dream was so real. Hearing him say, I love you was as if he was in the room with me. This has brought much pain of everything that I miss about Phil. I don't even want to write them down so as to prevent more pain.

What would I have told you Phil before I died, if it was me dying?

I just want everything to go back to how it was. I feel so angry.

I need to keep writing to get this anger and sadness out. Underneath all anger is sadness, frustration and hurt. All combined, these feelings are all with me.

It is all about coping with life on life's terms right now, without using anything to dull my pain. When the pain comes then I must write.

Friday September 30,

Today my mood has been flat and angry. The guy at the petrol station made me very angry, and I no longer want to be on my own. It is all about being on my own and all about me right now. It is coming up to six months now, and I just cannot believe it. I want it to all be over now. The novelty of my new house and new life is now over. I want my husband and friend back, my companion. I didn't ask for this God, why? I feel angry. I feel now is the time for it to be all about me.

This was the day that my anger reached a peak. It just bubbled over as I wrote and wrote about how angry I was. I even vented some of my anger to my therapist, David, by way of email. This was in fact very healing for me and I was grateful I could do this with him.

This email eventually dispersed my anger, and it enabled me to finally laugh and allow humour in to change my mood that day. It reminded me how important laughter was and that being in a state of gratitude for what I did have in my life was vital for turning around my thinking and of course, my mood.

One little quirk I have had was this desire to try and get through my life without ever using a petrol pump, only because it was something that I wanted to do, and in my forty one years I had still not pumped my own gas. Phil showed me how to fill up my car before he passed away, and whereas I told him that I was grateful for that, I was still going to try and never have to use one, simply because I had come this far, hence my frustration at the attendant at the petrol station that day, poor chap.

My email (and bad language) to David tells the story of my irrational feelings that day.

Hello there David....

Well, I am tired of this whole thing now. I no longer want to be a widow at forty one. I want my husband back. I am sick of the whole thing about being alone and having a life on my own, and I feel pissed off with everything! It is not fair, and I did not deserve this hand!

This morning the guy at the petrol pump really pissed me off. I don't do petrol pumps. The attendants idea of assistance was to show me how to do it. I wish I had the guts to tell him that I was not interested in being shown how to fill up my car. I don't do petrol pumps, and I never will. Instead I stood there and pretended to be interested on learning how to use a petrol pump. I will not be going to that station again. as I don't do petrol pumps, and I will return to my regular who fills it up for me. I was angry and disappointed in myself that I did not do my usual and simply drive away when I realized that no one was interested in filling up my car.

Can you tell that I am angry? Today I thought about what it would be like to get rid of this pain and anger by throwing down a whole lot of sugar. It wasn't an option actually, and I just accepted that right now my life sucks. I have every right to be angry about the cross I have been asked to carry. As if never having my own baby wasn't enough, I can't even have my own husband. It sounds as though I am feeling sorry for myself doesn't it? Well, actually, right now I do, and I am entitled to have this afternoon of self pity.

In writing this I think of my twenty eight year old friend who this afternoon is having a large cancerous lump removed from her breast, which has already spread into her lymph nodes. Whoever said that life was fair or would be easy? Today, what gives me joy is Fergus, who is feeling a tad better; my mother who constantly provides me with her loving ear; my home; and well, there is in fact a lot to be grateful for, even the friend who graciously reads this stuff. Enough about me. Let's talk about you, now. What do you think about me? On that note I will say good night.

To which David replied…

"What do I think of you? Well I think you are one of Creation's great gifts, and you are precious to all who know you. David C."

Well, thankfully today I had a good day in spite of things being tough and my rage boiling over. I am so tired now, possibly from all the emotion today. My email to David was very healing which actually really made me laugh and shifted my very angry and irrational mood. I then headed off to the gym which felt great and what an example of how your day, whilst it may start off difficult, does not have to continue that way and that you do have a choice. I must continue to remember that I can choose to be happy.

The time had now come to acknowledge the anger that was there for me, even though I was not sure at whom I was particularly angry at. Underneath my anger there was always sadness, frustration and fear.

Early on in my journey I had made the decision to do a good job of this grieving process, if there was such a thing. For me that meant really feeling it. The alternative may have meant I would not release myself to move on and possibly remaining stagnant in my life. This was not something that I wanted for myself, and just as importantly I knew that Phil would not want this for me. He was such an advocate for life.

I decided to really look into my methods of escapism, and it brought on deep reflection about the specifics of my body issues. I delved deeply into the meaning of what lay beneath the symptoms. These symptoms were, and always have been, simply the mask of the deeper issues and feelings that I was trying to escape. I decided to ask myself logical questions about the significance of some of these issues and why they were so important in my life.

I looked into my fears and the consequences of simply letting go of the restrictions and rules that I had placed on myself and imagined how life would be if these rules did not exist. Some of the questions that I asked myself were: what were my fears about becoming heavier, or too heavy for my liking? What were my fears about becoming too thin? How would being at a weight that I was happy with change my life? What space would this acceptance bring into my day, my thinking, my life? Why is it that the numbers that the scales say are so important to me? How can a simple number have so much influence on the state of my entire being that day? What would I replace this space with if I did not focus on this issue? What feelings would emerge if I in fact lived in the notion of total acceptance of myself on every level, not constantly striving to achieve and be perfect?

The feelings that I would have to face would be loneliness, sadness, anger, fear of my future and of course joy, which would probably be the most difficult emotion to accept at that point. How could I possibly feel joy again when I should be feeling constant sadness and despair, given my situation?

My parish priest, Father Cronin, was rather concerned about me when Phil first passed away, and when I mentioned to him that I was getting better and I had actually regained four or five kilos, his reply was, "Well, I suppose you are going to worry about that now are you." I replied simply with a laugh, aware of his sense of humour. Underneath that laugh though were my thoughts of "if he only knew how right he was." Somehow, I think he knew.

It was during these days when so much of my processing took place that once again I came to the familiar realization that I never allowed myself to stay in a place of complete acceptance of self. This I felt would be too painful. After all, how else could I escape my pain if I did not have something to divert my thinking to?

The relief that comfort eating gave me was only short term. For a few moments it would provide a temporary relief from whatever the uncomfortable feelings were that I was needing to escape from.

What followed would be incredible remorse, and, even though I was not one to indulge in large amounts of food, my thinking would shift into the place of not feeling accepting of my body and self. This kept me in that cycle of striving for the self acceptance that I had such difficulty in maintaining since my youth.

This stopped me from feeling true joy in my life which on some level I did not believe I was worthy of anyway, and besides joy did not last. This was my belief and it was too scary to let this belief go.

There were pages and pages of journaling and processing during this time. I made a commitment to myself and my wellbeing that no matter what, I would do my best to experience whatever feelings were present for me—to not run from my pain, my anger, nor my joy.

This also meant not projecting into my future, yet another mechanism I had learned, to escape from the present moment.

Whilst music was a healing tool for me, I found myself listening to the music at a blaring volume. It was fast, hurried and loud which did not welcome peace and calmness but another form of escapism. Therefore I was doing everything possible to slow down and feel, to be still and present, and see what eventuated with this different state of being, even if it was the simple action of changing the type and volume of music that I listened to.

What accompanied this commitment to self was of course deep pain. Old unresolved issues re-surfaced which I had to face again, such as the grief about not having my own baby. Things I thought I had put to bed were back again as this cleansing happened.

October was significant as it was the beginning of the anniversaries. Dates have always been important for me and what began for me now in my thoughts were the words this time last year. It was very difficult for me not to think about this. I was not willing to let it go, to let my past go. A part of me wanted to go back and recapture my life when Phil was alive, wanting to relive him as he was this time last year, even though he had already been diagnosed. At least he was still with me. I wanted to go back and feel what it was like still having him in my life.

Whilst I was very busy having commenced computer and counseling work again and recommencing studies, the loneliness was now beginning to hover. After all, it was the first time in many years that I was not part of a relationship.

The grief however had changed and was becoming less intense. I was having less occurrences of being crippled by the pain. Now it was the loneliness that would emerge, something I had not yet experienced. Often what would accompany this was my anger about the outcome of my life. Yes I am afraid to say that I had moments of feeling hard done by, not what I felt proud of. I never wanted to become a victim in this.

Monday October 3, 6 A.M.,

This morning I dreamt about Phil. He was happy and dancing around, and I wondered if his dancing in my dream was his way of telling me that he is now happy. I have been reflecting a lot on the confusion that existed for me during Phil's illness.

On the one hand I avoided the possibility that he might die. This thought was too unbearable to even contemplate, but it was also something that I was yearning to speak to him about, especially as I saw the physical changes in his body. My inner dilemma came about as my instinct kept pushing its way into my consciousness and whispering to me that he would not survive. Even when the hospice nurse came to visit us during the final weeks of Phil's life we both said, thank you for the offer for Phil to go into a hospice, but, no thanks. For Phil, accepting this would have been admitting defeat and surrendering what we held onto so dearly, which was our hope.

Wednesday October 5,

The weather is horrible. I feel quite lonely, and my days seem long. I have fallen into negative thinking and getting into the notion of there not being a lot to look forward to in my life now and about what a nightmare it would be one day to start a new relationship. I don't even go there. I look at a future on my own and that is what feels safest and easiest for me. In fact I often wonder if anyone could ever fill the shoes that Phil wore, so why would I even try? This is one area of my life that I just cannot even contemplate.

It is so important to keep away from such negative thoughts. This can then lead into such a decline in my feelings. I must keep my thoughts positive, keep feeling grateful for my life.

It is important to stay busy during these long summer nights. In fact, what on earth will I do with myself? I no longer have a garden to tend to or much housework to do, no one to cook for or take care of now, only Fergus. Mind you, he would not mind all that attention!

Actually I am bored, therefore this will be valuable time to heal, to study and to build my business again and of course my life, yes, to build *my* life now. This is yet another example to stay away from my stinking thinking and keep positive.

Some of the techniques I used to assist in my negative thinking were from Cognitive Behavioral Therapy, where I would attach my feelings to my thinking, and, by altering my thought pattern, assist in altering my feelings. Warning bells would sound when something physiological was happening for me, such as extreme fatigue, and often during these times my feelings would be low. These were signals for me that something deeper was going on and that the technique was necessary.

Thursday October 6,

Today the desire to cover up my feelings was there, and I did want to eat extra. What I did was call Cathy instead, and we had some great discussion about my process this week. My commitment this week was to feel the feelings, forget about my body size, to listen to my hunger and to trust my body. It knows best.

I need to experience what it feels like to be in my body when I am accepting of it, that is—how it feels to be completely accepting of my body: What possibilities does it open up for me? What does it mean for me spiritually, physically, emotionally, and professionally? How does it feel to be in that state of absolute self acceptance and love for self? Just imagine the possibilities for oneself if you were in this state every minute of the day, every day of your life. What on earth would ever hold you back in becoming the best that you can be? What would hold you back in finding your true self, your truth, your magnificence?

Each day I will be in that state and open myself up to the possibilities that this brings.

October 12, 2005, Six month Anniversary,

Today marks six months since Phil passed away. This grieving process is hideous. I observe myself trying to escape into the past or into anything to not feel the pain.

I recognize the need to release some of my guilt about the thoughts of moving on with my life, as I now want to on some level. This guilt though is such a difficult one to get through. What assists me is to reverse the situation and to think what Phil would want for me right now and what I would I want for him.

Today has been a good day, because my counseling went really well at Relationship Services. I am back doing what I should be doing at this time. It feels right for now, giving to others to get out of myself. It is providing me with some meaning and purpose in my life at this time, and I feel as though I am in the process of finding my own strength. Good does come out of tragedy.

Phil and I never spoke in depth about the possibility that he might die. We had only a brief sentence or two about it as we continued to live in hope. At times I needed to talk about it more, and I am sure that at times he must have also. Perhaps the timing was never right, and perhaps it was just too painful to even contemplate together. This was a subject which was to remain in our own hearts and not one we could share.

One of the things that I had never allowed myself to contemplate was the feeling of anger towards Phil. How on earth could I possibly be upset with my beloved whom had now passed away. This anger did arise for me, and thankfully it happened in the presence of my good friend Catherine who listened as my feelings were being released.

It was a couple of weeks later on October 21 when Catherine stayed over. We shared deeply and eventually I was able to voice what was so deeply embedded—namely, that as a result of Phil and I not speaking openly of his obvious fate, my healing had felt so incomplete and complicated.

That October evening I was able to admit to Catherine that I needed to speak to Phil then, and, whilst I was certain this was how Phil wanted it, to live in hope, on some level it was not what was best for me and left my wounds open. Phil wanted to protect me right up until the end and provide me with hope, so we did not speak of the possibility of him dying. It felt so incomplete for me. I felt robbed, empty by not having expressed my feelings to him about knowing that he was dying. There was unfinished business regarding the everydayness of life for me after he had passed—his funeral, my life, everything. Phil just could not speak of any of these things with me. On the other hand I understand why. It would have disrupted his own hope and blind faith. If I could turn back time would I do anything differently? "Absolutely not" would still be my answer. The one who is dying has to set the tone.

On this night my pain and anger had arisen, and my tears were long and heavy. On that night they felt justified, and I let them be released without guilt. This journey was hard for me, and I needed to acknowledge that. By the time I had awoken the following morning, my pain and anger had passed. All I needed was to release it as I had done the night before with Catherine.

Friday October 22,

It is now 2.40 A.M. Cathy is staying, and we had a lovely night together sharing so openly, which was great. She allowed me to open up and express feelings that I would not have normally allowed myself to express. Perhaps some of them I have kept hidden away and attempted to escape from by other means over the past few months. Last night I felt that I had the permission to express myself and there was no guilt attached.

Last night I realized that during my time of caring for Phil during the five months of his illness, I totally neglected myself. I did not care at all for my own well being. In fact, I wanted to die along with Phil and was hoping that by neglecting myself I would not last much longer either.

Instead of accepting a lot of the assistance that was offered, we both declined until those final weeks when we had no choice. We did not even want to part for the two nights when Phil went into the hospice, which was supposed to be a time of rest for me.

This is why I have felt so drained over the past months. I don't feel as though I have really stopped since his death. I have not allowed myself to do so, because it means the pain is often greater then.

Now, here I am six months later, still with these feelings that need to be dealt with. During Phil's final weeks I needed to have a conversation with him. I needed to speak of what I knew was a reality, but who was I to initiate such a conversation with him? Instinctively I just knew not to go there for Phil. He just wanted to protect me right up until that last day and live as if he was going to survive. That was how much hope he had and how much he loved me. Who was I to take that away from him? It was up to him to set the tone for his final act and no one else. At times I believe that he wanted to speak to me about death, but perhaps it was I who could not go there.

Phil, I am sorry for my anger. Sometimes I am not even sure what I am angry about or whom. I think you will understand.

October 24,

I have had 365 days of a nightmare. This day last year I had my last day of freedom from pain. You cannot help but go back to this time last year.

When I think of this as being forever, it is painful. I must remember to live only one day at a time. I cannot wait for this first year to be over, for his first anniversary to come, and go.

In spite of how busy I am, I feel lonely so I have made a decision to sit with my loneliness and work through it.

November I knew would be difficult. It was to be the first birthday of Phil's that I was to spend without him, and it would be the anniversary of the day of his diagnosis. Phil loved birthdays, especially his own and always made a big deal out of them and was never shy in saying that he loved getting presents.

As a significant date would approach, my anxiety would begin to arise and often my busyness would increase until the date arrived and left. I could not but help remembering him twelve months earlier on our cruise, "Honey, the only birthday present I want is to see another birthday next year."

As this day got nearer, I ensured that I was busy, busy and busier. This was what I did. Whether it be conscious or unconscious, once again I was racing. This was apparent in the nature of my journaling during those days. Not a lot of feelings were being processed—mainly the content of my day.

"Here I am in Phil's room, and I have not been coming in here much lately. Is it because it is too painful or is it because I am moving on? My emotions are changeable at the moment as Phil's birthday draws nearer."

November 8, 2005,

Today Phil would have been forty nine. I just want to race and get into my day and remain busy. I am not letting myself just sit and be. It is such a strange process. You just want to go through it as fast as possible so that you do not feel pain. Last night was not a great night's sleep in anticipation of what today would bring. I was awake a lot during the night. I had to see David C. today to get through. So be it, and I will do what it takes just to get through. Today I just needed the support.

November 20,

Today Ros and I went kayaking, something I have wanted to do for a while. I want to do different things now and let life be an adventure. Well, I managed to make a complete ass of myself as the first, well actually the only, person in the group to fall out. We were being taught how not to capsize your kayak and I, defying all the odds, had to fall out as I was practicing how not to! Consequently I froze and decided to cut the morning short. Oh well I was proud that I have once again stepped out of my comfort zone.

So much about life for me is now about filling it up with enjoyable things. There is such a void in my life now, and I once again have to rebuild and start from scratch on some level. Most importantly I must start filling the gap from within.

November 22,

A significant reading for me today….

Experience is not just the best teacher; it is the only teacher.

As we look back at our trials and hardships, we realize that, rather than being tragic and destructive, our difficulties have given us endurance, resilience, and patience. This is the direct outcome of going through trials. This is where hope comes from.

FIFTEEN

Goodbye 2005

Not only would December bring my first Christmas without Phil, it would also have been our ninth wedding anniversary and the anniversary of our first meeting on December 30 in 1994. All the significant dates were upon me, and as one arrived and went I would await the next one.

In spite of our telling each other every year that we would not buy gifts that year, neither of us could help it, and we would both rather guiltily present the other with our little surprise on the morning of our anniversary. On December 14 it seemed only natural that I go and buy myself an anniversary present. It was still a very tough day, and one where I greatly felt Phil's presence.

As much as I usually loved December and the festivities that came with it, I really did want this one to come and go. This feeling was such a double edged sword for me. I wanted to experience the joy of Christmas, but I also wanted to see the back end of 2005 so that I could then start using those most powerful words *last year.* I did make the effort and continued with my usual Christmas traditions of sending out cards, decorating my home and baking my Christmas cakes which I gave out as gifts. This actually was rather fun for me.

December 7,

Things are tough. I am lonely. I feel constant pain, and I am missing my mate. I am at the core of my grief and perhaps it is so much worse as Christmas is emerging. I am currently going through the idea of letting go of the need to grieve Phil. What does that mean for me? This I am not yet sure of.

On a positive note I have had quite a revelation over the past few days of my strength and belief in self. It is important that I trust my own intuition and always remember it is me who is the expert in my life and to always go within for answers.

December 25, 2005, Christmas Day,

This is my first Christmas without you Phil. Mass last night was beautiful. I loved the singing, the Christmas Carols and the hymns. I was so nervous about reading. My heart nearly came out of my chest, but I went up there and felt very proud. I could not look my family in the eye. Delwyn had tears and my mom too was having difficulty in holding in her pain.

Today I have had a good day, joyous even. In spite of having very little sleep, I was up at 5 A.M. and on an early walk with Carolyn. We were probably the only two people on the streets at this hour on Christmas morning. There was something special about it.

I was pottering at home most of the morning, preparing food, chatting on the phone and feeling happy with everyone and enjoyed all the well wishes from everyone who was thinking about me today. I have been given so many gifts this year for which I am so grateful, and I kept them all to open today.

It has been a beautiful family day at Zel and Delwyn's this year. We were all happy. My mom and dad came over with the intention of staying the night tonight. I did not want to be alone on Christmas night. I loved having them here, and we watched Rod Stewart in concert on DVD. It was great. Mom and I were bopping on the couch as dad desperately tried to sleep. By the end of the DVD I felt really happy. God bless my mom and dad. Their companionship had cheered me up enough to spend the night alone after all.

Wednesday December 28,

Today has been tough. I have been lonely and have sat with it. I can't say that today it is about missing Phil. It is about me being lonely, and there is a difference.

Yesterday I went for a squad swim on Takapuna beach, nearly froze to death, then arranged to go for a walk that day with one of the chaps from swimming, which we did along the waterfront. It was very pleasant, and it was lovely to have some male conversation and companionship.

What it brought home to me was that I was lonely and that I missed male companionship. I miss my cuddles from Phil, therefore I get them from Fergus.

December 31,

It is now 6.30 A.M., and here I am, the last day of the worst year of my life. This I can say for sure, and how have I passed through it I don't know. Well yes I do; most definitely it has been my faith that has seen me through—my trust in God. I must continue to trust—not necessarily know the plan but to simply trust it.

Can I look back and say that I wish I did anything differently? How could I even answer that question? I think as far as Phil goes I did everything perfectly as it was meant to be for him. I followed his lead and did as he wanted. Now it is time for me to do as I want in my life which is a hard thing for me to grasp, the notion of it now being *my* life.

New Years Eve is yet another milestone, another first without Phil and once again my sleep is not good. I am feeling very unsettled as this day emerges. It appears that anxiety arises for me until the date has passed, then I am good as gold.

It is now 11.40 P.M. on New Year's Eve. Fergus and I are snuggling up in bed together to see in the New Year together. I would not want it any other way tonight. Roll on 2006. I just want to see the back end of this year.

I have just been out for a barbeque, and whilst the company

was nice I felt a little out of place. It feels strange being single again. I needed to come home on my own to see in the New Year, with Fergus of course.

January 1, 2006 was like making a New Year's resolution. I wanted to purge 2005 and commence 2006 as if it was a new beginning for me. Somehow being able to say my husband died *last year* made Phil's death so much further away for me, even though it was only one day later.

The beginning of the New Year was exciting and enabled me to psychologically put the previous year behind me in some way. The power of those two words, last year, was incredible, even though I was still working through that first year and all of the firsts without Phil. The major ones had passed and now was the countdown to the first anniversary of his death.

I awoke on January 1 to the most glorious sunny day which in itself was enough to add to a joy that was already in my heart that morning. Last year was finally over for me. There was a real desire to create a vision for my life and have little goals along the way to achieve what I desired for myself. I felt excited that morning and a sense within that all would be well in my world.

January 1, 2006,

It is now 6.25 A.M. and once again Fergus and I are cuddling, the perfect way to see out the New Year and awake to the new one, with my faithful cat. My sleep was so much better last night, so I feel rested and alive today. Yesterday I let go and accepted what is, and this was truly freeing for me. This morning I awoke to a beautiful email from my brother Nick which brought emotion to me. How grateful I felt for my family:

Happy New Year My Darling Sister…

I could easily write for ages to you about all sorts of things, people, places, influences, highs and lows. Perhaps, that can wait for another day. Indeed, you'll be glad to see the back of 2005 and, miraculously, still have the courage to communicate with

God after all that's happened to you. A wee while ago I wrote suggesting that, perhaps, pennies would drop and all would become clear. You, immediately, wrote back demanding that a couple of bucks needed to fall out of the sky! Maybe I'm writing to remind you that they've already fallen, your health and loads of family and friends that really love you.

The (final) joyous pennies will drop when you feel the love and gratitude from those that you will help from your life coaching.

Meanwhile, stay away from ALL the Phil wannabe temptations. Don't bother going out with anyone unless they're prepared to scrape both knees (with gratitude) on the sidewalk while they're opening the car door for you.

Sveti Nikola xxx (Saint Nicholas)

This email still sits on my computer screen so that I can reflect on how profound his words were to me that morning, and still are.

Very early on January 1 I headed off for a walk along the Auckland waterfront with my music on, and I was on somewhat of a high. It felt such a joy in my heart as I powered along to a selection of songs I had put together on a CD.

One of my favorites at the time was a song which was based around Psalm 30. I had only discovered this fact after listening to it a couple of times, so this song became rather inspirational for me and gave me just as much strength as the Psalm itself did.

As I was walking this song came on, and I felt joy. At that present moment all was well in my world, and I was singing away feeling rather grateful. At that moment from a distance I could see something in the sky coming towards me and as it came closer I realized that it was a lone bird. Normally I would not notice something like this, however what brought it to my attention was that it was coming towards me at a rather rapid pace, so much so that I remember thinking to myself that soon I would have to duck or else this stupid bird was going to hit me as it was flying directly towards my face.

In order not to get torpedoed by this bird, I had to stop on the footpath, and then suddenly this bird also stopped and landed right in front of my feet. At that moment my heart nearly burst from my then beating chest as I realized it was a white dove.

Tears immediately filled in my eyes as I leaned down towards this dove as it walked around my feet. It was not fearful of me at all. It felt as though this dove was there to say, *you will be alright; just trust.* Nothing could have held my tears back that morning and I am sure that to a passerby I probably appeared like someone who would have had too much of the New Years Eve cheer the night before. Yes, I was drunk—I was drunk on joy, sadness and gratitude as the words of the song continued in my ear, "Weeping may go on all night but in the morning there is joy."

To some, events like this may not mean a lot, but to me on that morning what I felt was special and it was yet another example of being shown that I was being held, that my life would be happy and Phil was indeed also joyful.

One can call it a sign, synchronicity, whatever. I just knew that I was safe and felt happy to move forward with my life. Deep within me I knew that I had Phil's blessing to let go of my pain, whatever letting go meant for me, which perhaps I was still trying to define.

January 2,

Today I am feeling good. It is important that I have to be still and listen. That can be a little difficult. I am tired of being at home so much now, and it does get lonely. I am ready to start socializing a little more, going out, even dressing up again.

Life is so short. That I know for sure, therefore I now want to live this life to the fullest. What are some of the things I want to do this year? I want to be more spontaneous and have more fun, spend quality time with my friends. Here I am planning a future on my own, no more planning with Phil, and it all feels fine, not scary. It feels good to know that I will be working more again one day and that I will write my book and begin building my career and my new life.

During the next few days my writing was very much content of what was happening in my day. There was not so much an expression of my grief. I was now getting on with my life and making plans. I was starting so socialize more with friends and getting excited about getting out of the house.

Slowly I was beginning to have coffee with a couple of male friends and that felt very strange for me. Although there was no attraction at all, it still felt scary for me and reminded me how I did feel insecure about being a single woman in the big wide world. Was there a stigma attached to being single? Did it have an influence on my feeling of value in the world? Did I need to be in a relationship in order to feel valued? All of these questions were arising for me. I did feel vulnerable, however I did not realize how vulnerable I was until some months later.

Sunday January 22,

My weekend has been great. Friday night I got dressed up and went out for Carolyn's birthday. It was good to get myself done up, but it was rather strange going on my own and entering a restaurant on my own. I felt as though I had a sign on my head saying widow.

It is now 9.15 P.M., and I am in bed after having a spin with my nephew in his old souped-up Mercedes which was such a laugh. I went out my front door in my pajamas and drove around town for a while. Zel was in the front seat laughing. Xavier, Nicholas and I were in the back seat, and handsome Alexander was driving, cruising around with his elbow out the window. It was such a scream, and I felt so happy. I cannot believe that I am feeling so happy on my own as I venture out of my comfort zone to be a little more spontaneous with things.

Today Michelle and Owen brought over my bike. I was so excited about now attempting a triathlon. I ended up going for a big walk to Mission Bay in the sunshine which was great, and I feel excited about my life now. I am really embracing it, doing everything that I can.

Why the joy; am I forgetting that I will be without Phil forever whilst on this earth?

Today I read my diary of love letters from Phil. May that always remind me of what I had and that I would not ever settle for anything less...ever. It really does make me wonder if I will ever allow myself to be happy with a man again.

Sunday February 12,

"Well it has been ten months since Phil passed away, and once again I am struggling with the reality of this today, and I desperately want him back. The horror just appears from nowhere and hits you when you least expect it.

Today I have exercised far too much, and I am feeling out of balance in my life at the moment. My foundation has been shaken. I am doing everything to the extreme, so I think I am feeling fatigued from all the exercise for this triathlon."

Friday February 17, 11.10 P.M.,

It is now around the same time that Phil died. I am still not able to forget about dates and times. Will I ever? Tonight I went out for a meal and drinks with a friend in Herne Bay, not far from where Phil and I used to live. I actually had a fun time with her, and we met up with others whom I knew, and it was nice to get dressed up to go out for a summer's night.

I found it difficult driving home late at night on my own though. I really felt the loss of Phil and my aloneness. I feel rather uneasy and vulnerable in the world. It feels safe in my home. and it would be very easy to become reclusive and not venture out.

Saturday February 18,

Last night driving home, I felt alone, and I missed Phil. To top it off I came home to no Fergus, and he did not come home for quite a while. The fear took over, and I felt the loss of Phil as I built this enormous scenario inside of losing Fergus. Where was he?

I knew that it was irrational thinking. He was probably out gallivanting around, terrorizing some poor other cat, however this panic and anxiety came over me that crippled me like I had not felt for some time. I could not bare the thought of him not coming home. I could not bare the thought of yet another loss.

He showed up a few hours later and very happy with himself. I was simply relieved to have him home.

Sunday February 27,

Tonight I feel sad. I feel as though I have let Phil go on some level. I am not sure if it is guilt I feel or what. There is a knowing that I must let go of this need that I have to grieve, another *should* in my life.

Phil was such an honest man. He did not have a cunning or manipulative bone in his body. He was such a beautiful human being, and how honored I feel to have been his wife. However, it feels time to now let go, whatever that means for me.

SIXTEEN

A Time for Reflection

It became very apparent to me that I was not able to keep up with the schedule and demands that I was placing on myself. In hindsight, deciding to do a triathlon was probably something that I used, to distract myself from the first anniversary of Phil's death which was to be within days of the triathlon. This meant that I would need to exercise more, which I loved. This however proved to add to my busyness and created more fatigue which led to my moods also being affected—yet another way the grief manifested itself.

One could not tell me this though. I wanted to fit everything into my life. At times I felt as though I was a child in a candy store, with so much to choose from, taking a bit of everything and not really knowing where to start chewing first, or how many to put in your mouth at one time. I had given myself permission to rebuild my life, to experience as much as I could, and, whilst I had recognized the need to let go of the busyness, it still did not stop me from putting far too much on my plate.

Something had to give and sure enough it was my body. On a run one day I hurt my knee and within days I was not able to walk—thus a forced halt to the idea of the triathlon.

Hurting my knee was a catalyst to slow me down physically, to come off this cycle and to simply to *be*. I knew it all but putting it into practice was often so difficult for me. Being a *doer* I was not one to sit and rest unless my body was so exhausted that it could do no more.

Phil's anniversary was getting closer, and I wanted to make it a momentous occasion. I recall when his friend Kevin passed away, Phil and I were sitting up in bed on the evening of the first anniversary of his death, and Phil said to me that "one year was long enough to have as an official mourning period. I will never forget him, however it is time to let him go, let him be on his next journey."

During this time I remembered these words, and I always felt that Phil wanted me to slowly begin to let go of more of the physical so that I could find my own way in life and not hold onto something that could no longer be.

As April 12 slowly came closer and was within my reach, I knew on a deep level that Phil was there with me, assisting me to find my true meaning in letting go and to slowly do it. Some say that I had taken too long, that I should have let go of his ashes sooner, or distributed his clothing sooner, or not had my little shrine to Phil still there, but I knew this process had to all happen in my time and no one else's.

During the weeks leading up to Phil's anniversary I had made the decision that this would be a time of remembrance, of quiet reflection of Phil, of our life, of our journey over the past eighteen months and of preparing myself to let the physical go. It needed to be my time again, just as it was on April 12 one year earlier. Whilst I wanted us to come together on the day of Phil's anniversary to celebrate him again, being alone during the weeks leading up to that date was important for me and was what I chose to do. I accepted very few social engagements, spent many hours on my own with the physical that was left of Phil and once again, grieved.

March 4, 2006,

Tonight I have had a long chat with Shirley, my very wise friend who always gives me so much encouragement. I have had a big cry, and this is what she has told me all of which I wrote down:

"Don't feel guilty about moving on. There is no muddle for you Tanya. Be aware of the muddy water. I see a beautiful wine shaped glass with a long stem. It is beautiful. The hardest thing that you will have to deal with is that the angels are offering you this glass. Don't run and hide; be strong. There is no need for you to flounder around in the muddy waters. There is triumph for you and Phil. The glass is being handed to you, so be bold. We want your shoulders back, well done true and faithful servant. This is a Heaven given glass with no muddy water. Move on quietly with direction. Keep your eyes wide open, senses clean and clear. You don't need people around to commiserate. There is triumph. Phil has triumphed. Quietly move on, one tiny step forward. Cry into your cup given to you from heaven, not into the muddy water. Crying into the muddy water will sink. Give me wisdom. Into your heaven given glass, every tear is counted and heard. Ask. Give of yourself, but you have to go to the right place to be fed. You have a heaven-given strength. Peace, love and kindness vs. fear and anger. Which one will win? The one you feed will win. Which one will I feed? Guilt is the muddy water. See how beautiful you are Tanya."

I read something beautiful today about prayer: "Fill up your emptiness with prayer. Do not allow emptiness inside of you, but fill this emptiness with prayer. Prayer is the best medicine to defend your heart against sadness."

It is now 8 P.M., and I have been on the couch for three hours now, and I am feeling really well. I have worked through so many of my feelings. It is so necessary that I live in the present moment and let no person, no situation, no holiday, nothing external to fulfill me at that deep level. I need to go within. It is my relationship with myself that matters most.

If one day someone else comes into my life, he will simply enrich my life, two lives joined together, rather than one taking over the other. My life is so good now. Why on earth would I enter into something with another person if his presence did not in fact enrich my life and I his? What would be the point?"

Sunday March 12,

Today marks eleven months since Phil went to Heaven.

Once again I am alone a lot at the moment which I don't mind at all. Actually I am enjoying the rest. It feels like everything has settled, me in my new home, life in general, and the reality that Phil died. I know that sounds a bit harsh, but that is what is. Life as I knew it will never return and now it is time to bring on my new life.

Trying to recall my old life will not bring it back. Trying to recall my memories of Phil will not bring him back; time to let go. It is also time to clear out Phil's clothing I feel. There is nothing social happening in my life, and I want to keep it that way until Phil's anniversary. it needs to be a quiet time of reflection for me. I need to trust that, in time, my life will change, but for now I want to stay on top of my studies and *be* with whatever comes. Actually I feel so much joy in my heart right now as I sit quietly…in the now!

March 23,

Today has been a good day. In fact all days are good when I practice self care. I have not exercised all day, and it feels great. I don't really feel lonely, although I do miss Phil and sharing my life with him. Right now I am not interested in anyone else. My life is very full, and that is how I would like it to stay. I like being on my own. The thought of ever being in a relationship one day seems just too hard.

Last night I was dreaming that I was scattering Phil's ashes at the Rose Gardens at the place where we had our photos taken by the arch of white climbing roses, so I have decided this is what I will do on his anniversary.

Whilst scattering Phil's ashes on his anniversary felt like the right thing to do, I was also aware that the time was approaching, and soon I would have to let go of the physical of Phil that I had so desperately held onto over the past twelve months.

As April 12 approached my anxiety began to rise. I was unsure of how this day would be for me. What would it really mean? There was also another part of me that wanted this date to come and go. Perhaps then I would be able to give myself permission to let go a little more and live. During these weeks it would not take much to trigger my grief. This notion of letting go was with me, and, one morning in late March as I walked towards the Rose Gardens, I could feel my tears building. It was midmorning, once again the most glorious sunny autumn day, just as it was the year before, Indian Summers as Phil would refer to them as. As I arrived at the Rose Gardens I looked to the right to the arch where two white climbing roses were still blooming. The names of the roses I felt were so appropriate, *White Knight* and *Peace.*

It was in between this arch that Phil and I stood, as husband and wife and had our photos taken on our wedding day. As I looked across to where this event took place nearly nine years earlier, and where in a few days another significant event would take place, I felt this stabbing in my heart, disbelief and an excruciating feeling of loss. How could this be, I thought to myself through my tears. I continued walking, and within seconds I looked to the left, and my eyes immediately went to the number plate of a car, parked directly outside the Rose Gardens. It read JCMYM8, and, written in words above and below the numbers, it said, *Jesus is my mate, is he yours?*

My heart leapt. These were the words that Phil spoke to me just moments before he died, that "Jesus is my mate." I smiled and said, "Oh Phil, yes, you did say that Jesus was your mate. Thank you; thank you for showing me again that you are happy and that you are with me." My tears then turned from those of mourning into tears of joy as I felt him more than I can describe to you with these words. I felt his presence. My darling Phil was dancing, and this was what he also wanted me to do.

As the Psalm promised, "Weeping may endure for the night, but in the morning there is joy." How could I ever doubt that I was taken care of? This occurrence gave me so much joy, and I continued to walk, knowing, that if I but truly asked and listened, I would be led.

That morning I did not feel I was being silly and simply looking for signs. I felt a sense of peace in my heart which was a gift, and there was nothing more for me to say or explain to anyone.

April 2, 6.35 A.M.,

Here I am in bed listening to the rain pelt down. Thank God I am not doing that triathlon. Poor Michelle is still going to do it. I could not imagine anything worse on a day like today.

Yesterday was a lovely day at my cousin's wedding. In spite of being rather difficult being at the first wedding on my own, I could not help but reflect as I watched this couple coming together for life being reminded of what I no longer had, but it was manageable for me and I had a great night.

Everything feels good actually. I am now ready to let some of Phil's things go such as his possessions, his clothing. I am even looking forward to April 12. It feels like time.

During this time I began to remove Phil's clothing from what was still Phil's room. some I distributed to a family who were willing to wear it, some of his beautiful suits were given to a couple of his friends, and the remainder I carefully bagged up and gave to St Vincent de Paul society.

As I was kneeling on the ground in his little room, carefully laying the suits out, taking as much care as I could and slowly zipping up the suit carrier, for an instant the vision of Phil's face was there. It brought me back to that night, nearly 365 days ago when I was very carefully preparing his body to be taken away, slowly folding the white sheet around his very still body.

My face fell into my hands as I began to weep at the thought of what I had lost. I was slowly letting go, removing from my home those physical things of Phil which a part of me still wanted to hold but also so desperately wanted and needed to now let go of.

April 10,

It is early and here I am now again in Phil's room, and I feel quite taken back by the smell of the candles. It is such a reminder of those same candles burning around his casket. The anniversary is getting closer now, and I only have Phil's ashes for a little longer. It does feel like time.

It is hard for me to explain what my pain is about, the letting go, living without him, letting go of our dreams, and I am really not sure. What I do know is reaching this mark will be significant for me. I know that I will continue to feel joy in my life and that I will be truly happy again.

It is now the evening, and what a day today has been. The pain today is simply sorrow, simple sadness and grief. I miss him so much. I know that I am letting go. Tonight I placed his shirts and suits into the suit carrier. As I zipped them up it reminded me of that night when I was covering Phil's body.

Lord I know that I must go through this pain for now and that soon it will pass. Help me. Remember me.

On the day before Phil's anniversary, I began to clear out his room, and soon it would become my room. I had put away all of the memorabilia of Phil, and all of his clothes were now gone. What was left were the two boxes which contained his ashes, and on top was a beautiful photo of Phil.

It was important to me that when I awoke on April 12, all was to be cleared, apart from some candles which were surrounding his ashes, which would then be taken that evening.

April 12 was a glorious day, with not one cloud in the blue sky, which seemed to go on forever. I awoke feeling peaceful and rather excited at the thought of what today would bring knowing the significance it had for me. This day was a ritual I had planned for weeks and was something that I needed as part of my process of moving forward.

Mass was arranged to be said for Phil that day at the same church where he was given his final farewell. Early that morning I made my way early to the church and was thrilled that so many others came to celebrate Phil again on that day. Monsignor Cronin reminisced about Phil, and again I proudly read, really wanting to be strong for Phil on this, his and my, special day.

After mass some of us had breakfast together. We all laughed and sat in the hot autumn sun. I felt happy, and I also noticed how happy my mom was that morning. As we drove away together we shared how strong and at peace we both felt. There was no room for tears that day, and somehow we had a knowing that Phil was dancing.

The rest of that day I spent quietly on my own in what was still Phil's room.

Here I am in Phil's room. I have just prayed the Rosary and had quiet time this afternoon, just sitting with his remains one last time. I feel ready to let them go. What a superb day it has been. The love of the Lord is great.

On the evening of April 12 my family came to be with me as did Phil's brother-in-law Neil and Catherine had come to stay the night with me so that I was not alone. We were all laughing and joyous together as the day had been so beautiful thus far. However as the evening came and the darkness arrived, my anxiety began to build as the time was coming near, to finally let go.

What was now happening for me was the awareness that soon I would not have Phil's remains here, that soon I would not have his box of ashes to kiss goodnight, as I had done every night now for close to one year.

I cannot recall who finally had the courage to say to me that it was time. I too, still wanting to delay the inevitable, knew it was. Alone I went up to Phil's room. I stood at the dresser which was tall enough so that when I looked at these boxes with the ashes, they were close to eye level. I began to speak to Phil, and once again I said goodbye. My tears that had not been with me all day had finally arrived as I reached over, removed the boxes and cradled them into my chest. At that point I did not want to let him go, but I knew that I had to. I knew that Phil wanted me to. I knew that I must.

Slowly I carried them from the room, my tears falling long and hard at this point, and up the stairs came my brother Antoni cuddling me and telling me that it would all be well as I knew it would. My heart however was still breaking.

When we reached the bottom of the stairs, my first vision was my mom who at this point was also weeping. Mom did not want to come to the Rose Gardens. She chose to stay behind, so I was joined by all of my brothers, my dad, Neil and Catherine as we made our way in the dark with Phil to his final resting place. By the time we reached the gardens, my tears had been and gone, and once again I felt a peace and a knowing that it was time and that I had Phil's blessing.

The ashes were surprisingly heavy. He filled up two boxes in fact. Between all of us, Phil was scattered amongst the two climbing roses, Peace and White Knight, and also amongst a deep bed of red roses called Firelight, where his parents remains were also scattered. The final stage in Phil's journey was now complete, and for me a chapter had now closed.

When we returned home that night it was just Catherine and I for the rest of the evening, just sharing. With both of us exhausted, we wanted to wait up until the time Phil passed away at approximately 11:11 P.M.

I was sitting on the couch with Fergus as he lay outstretched on my lap and was keeping an eye on the time and looking at the candles which had been burning all day by Phil's photograph. The time got closer. Catherine's tears were now falling, and, as she approached the candle by Phil's photo, they came harder and louder, and it was she who extinguished this candle at 11:11 P.M.

April 13, 2006, 7.30 A.M.,

Phil is now gone from this room. His ashes are now gone. What remains is his photograph and one of his *mate,* Jesus, and mother Mary. It feels so empty in here now, very much like those days just after his funeral, after his body was gone from the house. The lounge then became so cold and empty.

I feel rather empty now. Everyone has gone and now life returns to normal. The question for me now is what is normal?

Everything about Phil's journey and my journey to date was perfect. We prayed for a miracle, and I believe that miracles have been delivered. Today's reading in my little book is all about continually giving thanks, and that I will always do.

Seventeen

Moving Forward

There was an immense freedom for me once April 12 had passed, and, just like January 1, twenty-fours made a huge difference to my thinking and how I felt.

Such a vast difference to the need I had of holding onto my grief in those early months, it was as if I did not want to let the world see that I was actually healing and had found a willingness to live again. Finally after April 12 I had released myself from the self-imposed prison that was created in my own mind.

April 14, 2006, Good Friday,
    In spite of finding it hard to not keep thinking about this time last year, here I am, ready and willing to live my life. When Phil passed I could not imagine how I would function without him. I now see that I have in fact been doing that. One day at a time, I will continue to live, to find meaning in my experiences and feel gratitude for what I now have in my life.

April 15, 2006,
    Today I awoke early, and here I am now in my little room, and I feel fine. Every now and then the permanence of not having Phil in my life does hit me, but I cope. Thankfully, the rest of my life is fantastic. In fact there is so much to be grateful for.

There is a difference for me now in letting go of Phil's ashes and reaching the one year mark. I feel more open and free to be happy. There is greater acceptance. The pain is manageable, and I now reflect on the good memories we had.

I found another beauty today during my readings. "I must keep calm and unmoved in the vicissitudes of life. I must go back to the silence of communion with God to recover this calm when it is lost even for one moment. I will accomplish more by the calmness than by all the activities of a long day. At all cost I will keep calm. I can solve nothing when I am agitated."

April 16, 2006, Easter Sunday,

What an awesome dream I have just awoken from. I was in church, and on the altar I saw Phil up there with his arms wide and giving me the thumbs up, and he was laughing. It was so cool, and it made me happy. I hope that is how it is for him. Well I have to believe that it is. The vigil Easter Mass last night was superb. Carolyn came and it was great to have her there. This morning I feel joyful. I don't really have any worries right now. In fact, what part of my life do I worry about? None really, I trust that all is taken care of.

In spite of my greatest loss. This is how God wants to use me, to show people how through faith you can endure anything, and, by not being afraid to express my faith, I can honestly share how my journey has been. This provides me with purpose and meaning in my life, and I must continue to remember this.

One day at a time, I can calmly cope with whatever is presented to me."

April 20,

It is early. Here I am now in my little room having my quiet time, and I feel very happy. What a gift this is to feel excitement about my life again.

What do I want to do with my life? Why am I doing what I am doing in my life? Ultimately for me, as Phil so beautifully put it one day, "Tarn, this is God teaching me that it is not all about the physical but the spiritual."

Lately I have been reflecting about how the pain does diminish. The tsunamis are less intense and further apart. In the early days when people would tell me that time heals. I wanted to throttle them, however it is true. There is an unexplained difference for which I am grateful. I feel as though I have thrown myself into the grief over the past year. It was what I needed to do.

Now there is a real willingness for me to live my life. This is just such an awesome feeling. I only hope that I know how to. No doubt I will still get hammered, but that no longer scares me. I accept it all as part of the process. It would not be natural if the tsunamis did not still come. The difference now is that I am up there riding them and not being drowned by them, perhaps a slight dunking but nothing too bad I believe.

Now is the time to have a bit more of a social life. I am getting a bit housebound, cabin fever I think they call it. There is now a need to write my book, which I will now do, and I believe that it is time for me to now dance as Phil would want me to.

Being alone is tough at times. Thankfully my life is full, and I have wonderful friends, and there is so much living to do. Often I miss a companion but all in good time. It is too early for me. Just some male company would be nice. In spite of this loneliness, I do feel very grateful and blessed for my life. I feel so fortunate.

Thank You God for my life…. Thank You for healing my sorrowful heart.

May 5, 2006 was a day that was painful yet also triumphant for me on many levels. My mom had a recurrence of an existing heart condition which was bad enough for her to be admitted to Auckland Hospital, and it was the first time in just over a year since April 12 that I had entered this building.

It took some months after Phil's death that I was actually able to directly look at this building when I drove past as it is so close to my home.

My anxiety arose as I entered the ward where mom had been admitted, and immediately I realized that it was exactly the same ward where Phil was admitted just over one year ago and where he was told by that doctor with the graying beard that he would not be leaving the hospital alive.

All of my memories returned to me in an instant. I had gone back in time to once again relive the horror of April 12 the year before.

It was when I found the area where my mother lay, that took my breath away. She looked so helpless there with her oxygen mask on. "Oh God no," I thought to myself, not another oxygen mask as it was Phil's face I saw behind that mask, not my mother.

Standing still as I held her hand, was impossible for me as wanting to cry. I saw her fear, just as I saw Phil's fear. It pained me to see this fear again. "Please don't look at me Mom with those blue eyes, please."

Whenever mom would enter the hospital on these occasions, I found the strength to comfort her, to be strong for her, just as I did for Phil. She came first, just as Phil came first. This time however there was no strength in me. I could not sit still, constantly getting up, walking around, pacing, trying to calm myself. It felt as though I was placed in an abyss and could not find my way out.

Everyone and everything was agitating me. I was suffocating amongst all these walls. All these people, all these monitors, don't any of you know how I feel? I needed to get out and get out fast. I had not experienced this feeling before.

As I paced, I found a bathroom. It was a large cubicle. They are all shaped the same, and again it felt like the same bathroom in which I made phone calls from some thirteen months ago. Another memory was crashing at me that just would not stop. I glanced at myself in the mirror and saw pain and fear as the tears came, my face red with tension as this woman once again was staring back at me wondering why on earth this was happening again in my life.

Not knowing where to turn I phoned David Chaloner, and thankfully he answered his cell phone. He allowed me to fall apart, to share my pain and my anger that once again I was in this hospital in this situation, and at that moment I was not coping with any of it. David allowed me to weep and once again feel my grief of watching my husband take his final breaths only thirteen months earlier in that same ward, the memories of which all seemed so fresh to me at that present moment.

Logically I knew that my mother would not die. What I was reliving was in fact past pain and fear—something that I needed to face again in this building so that it did not have that power over me. I knew that my mother needed me, so I wiped the tears from my face and heard David's words to me which were that yes, I now had a job to do for my mother, just as I had thirteen months earlier for Phil.

Shortly afterward I was again at my mother's side. Within hours her heartbeat had returned to normal, her condition was stable, and in time she would make a full recovery. For a while it was just the two of us, and by that stage I was able to sit and be there for her.

Mom was moved into a room where she would spend the night and rest, which allowed me to return home. Just before I left, I realized that this room was directly across from the exact room that Phil lay just hours before he died.

This was the room where Phil received his final communion and blessing from Mons Cronin. It was the room where he said goodbye to my parents, my brother Nick, our friends Lois and Allan. It was the room where he looked at me constantly with those deep blue eyes, where they followed my every step and where he looked at me as I leaned over him and said that we needed to believe in miracles.

I knew I had to face this room, therefore at its entry I stood, without moving, my arms folded and head looking at the empty bed there, remembering Phil, those luscious blue eyes that radiated perfection, those eyes that radiated love.

Again I mourned. Quietly within I said goodbye again to Phil, knowing that this day was a turning point for me, more letting go of the horror of that final night.

Returning home that night without Phil was easier. I was returning to my home which had no memories of Phil or the cancer. Catherine once again was there for me as I stood at my kitchen bench sharing, crying, screaming as once again grief enveloped me. I was enraged at the world that here I was again having to endure such pain. She listened, responded softly as only Catherine knew how and allowed me to process the feelings that were literally erupting from the depths of my being.

This night was like having an emotional enema and would be a major turning point for me in many areas of my life. Upon my return from the hospital that night I wrote the following:

> It is now 8.30 , and I am in bed totally exhausted. What a day, I totally surrendered my day to You Lord, and I felt such a peace. Then all this happened—mom in hospital, reliving this pain again, the worst day for such a long time.
> Lord, it is time for me to live my life now. Help me and show me. I gave my day to You today, yet it was very difficult. Is there still more learning for me? If so, please show me.

The following day was yet another experience of letting go for me, of my attachments, my need to rescue, my need to care for others, my need to carry burdens that were not mine. That day a feeling of empowerment was surrounding me more than I had ever experienced in my life…Tanya, the strong, adult woman had emerged and had finally taken centre stage in her life and was about to commence it with unstoppable enthusiasm. I felt like this light beaming in the world, and more importantly I was not afraid for it to shine or to be seen by others as shining, in the hope that their's also would ignite. The difference now was that I would not be doing it for them; they were to do it for themselves if they chose to.

There was such a joy in my heart that afternoon, and once again I shared with Catherine at length about my willingness to live my life now, to let everything and everyone go. There was a sense of gratitude to Phil. Deeply I believed that he was a guiding light for me during this entire process of letting go and living now without guilt attached.

On my way to mass that afternoon, I stopped at the Rose Gardens where I could still see pieces of Phil's remains lying on the ground below those white climbing roses, and my words to him were, "Thank you; you are a man of your word. You said that you would be my angel, and that you are."

It was difficult to believe that less than twenty-four hours earlier I was engulfed with the most agonizing of pains, yet at this present moment there was joy and dancing in my heart, just as the Psalm promised.

Saturday May 6, 2006,

Thank You Lord. With You, my life feels joyful.

Psalm 30 is very much with me, "Weeping may go on all night but in the morning there is joy. He has made me steady as a mountain. Then he turned my sorrow into joy. He took away my clothes of mourning and clothed me with joy, so that I might sing glad praises to the Lord, instead of lying in silence in the grave. Oh Lord my God, I will keep thanking you forever." It is now the evening and my trusted mate Fergus is now snoring rather loudly on my lap. Tonight at the Rose Gardens I thanked Phil for my learning and getting me through the past few days, and once again I asked to feel some of the joy that he is feeling in Heaven right now, and sure enough it came. I am now ready to live.

Our first photo together at Phil's brothers wedding in February 1995.

December 14, 1996. I was very happy to become Phil's wife and Phil was very happy to become 'Philipovich'!

Phil with his cat Chi. Rarely was there a time when Chi was not draped on Phil's body somehow, some way.

Phil loved the horses. A typical spring Saturday often involved gardening and betting on the races.

Phil had a wonderful dry sense of humour.
Here he is welcoming the young man who delivered our
Indian takeaways by acknowledging his culture
in his best Indian attire.

Always there with a laugh with his sister Marie
and myself at yet another family get together
to celebrate their birthdays.

Phil with
brother-in-law.
Neil.

A favourite
photo of us
at a wedding.
February 2002.

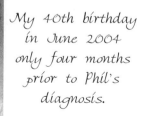

My 40th birthday
in June 2004
only four months
prior to Phil's
diagnosis.

The weekly Saturday morning gym workout and breakfast with the boys. Apparently stomach workouts were not necessary due to all the laughter around the table.

Phil flirting with the girls in Jamaica November 2004. We had a wonderful day and were able to forget our sorrow.

Dressed up to celebrate Zel's 50th birthday in Paris.

From left, Zeljana, Xavier, me, Zel, Delwyn and Dominique.

My faithful buddy and office assistant Fergus.
Note the blanket especially for him with prime views!
He was by my side during the many hours
of writing this book.

Celebrating my 43rd birthday in June 2007.
My awesome brothers Nick, Antoni and Zel.

*With my wonderful parents in October 2007
and I am smiling again.*

*December 2007 with brother Zel.
I threw a 'coming out party' to celebrate myself as a
woman finally content with who I am.*